MY GEMS
William M. Harnett
National Gallery of Art, Washington, D.C.
Gift of the Avalon Foundation

Mary B. Huss

From Beth
Christmas '77

Your
Lhasa Apso

By Dr. Robert J. Berndt

Compiled and Edited by
William W. Denlinger and R. Annabel Rathman

DENLINGER'S
Box 189, Fairfax, Virginia 22030

Pictured on the front cover is Ch. Ruffway Mashaka, with Georgia Palmer, breeder-owner-handler, and Dr. Robert J. Berndt, judge. On the back cover is Ch. Maytime Genghis Khan in a non-show pose, with the hair pulled back to show the expression.

Foreword

This book is offered as a study of the Lhasa Apso. A product of Tibet, the Lhasa Apso is gaining yearly in popularity both as a show dog and as a family pet. In an effort to help the new dog owner, this book offers chapters on the Lhasa Apso's personality, his care and feeding, and his place as a member of the family.

This book is a result of the experiences gained by the Author in working with the breed for more than a dozen years as a breeder, exhibitor, and judge. It is a pooling of the knowledge offered by other breeders during this period of time. Acknowledgement is here made of the contributions of the many exhibitor-breeders who have shared their knowledge, their records, their photographs, and their time in bringing this volume to publication. A special thanks is given to Dr. Bernice Warren, who read the original manuscript and made numerous editorial suggestions.

R. J. B.

RJB Jane going
Winners Bitch
with Owner-Handler
Dr. Robert J. Berndt.

Contents

Five-month-old RJB Glen and RJB Greta.

Maytime Tristan and Maytime Galahad at six weeks of age.

Selecting the Lhasa Apso Puppy

The decision to purchase a dog is always a major one, and one that brings with it a great deal of excitement, whether it is the selection of the first family pet or the addition of a new show dog for a major kennel. In either case, considerable study and preparation should be made before the decision becomes final.

For the moment, only those problems involved in acquiring a family pet will be presented, with a later section of the book devoted to the concerns of show-quality dogs.

Purchasing a pet can become a good family project for the children. It can be a learning experience necessitating trips to the public library to study about the various breeds and their suitability as members of the family. The family that is serious about selecting the right breed and the exact specimen should take several trips to well-established breeding kennels and should attend at least one dog show to see examples of the breed at various ages from puppyhood to full adulthood. This will help to prevent the development of the shocks that might occur as a tiny, cuddly puppy grows into an oversized, unmanageable dog.

Once all the preliminary steps have been taken, and all family discussion has led to the decision to buy a Lhasa Apso, then a reputable kennel should be selected for the purchase. If there is a local kennel club and it has a kennel referral service, the problem is simplified. However, since many localities do not have such a service available, it might be necessary to consult one of the national magazines devoted to dogs. These magazines usually contain classified ads arranged in a geographical index which will simplify finding a kennel within easy driving distance. There are a number of serious breeders located across the country who are dedicated to the betterment of the breed and will make a great effort to help the prospective buyer find just the right puppy.

A pet-quality Lhasa Apso puppy will cost between one hundred and two hundred dollars. It may be possible to find a half-grown dog even somewhat cheaper, although this may not be a good buy, for it is sometimes more difficult for the dog to make the necessary adjustment when six months of age. A great deal will depend on the personality of the individual dog.

In larger cities the classfied section of the newspaper will have a column advertising pets for sale. This is also a valuable source of information and a possible means through which to find a kennel. Commercial pet shops located in shopping centers frequently have a large selection of various breeds readily available. Most pet shops will sell pets on time payments, which makes them especially attractive to some prospective buyers.

Most pet shop owners do not breed their own dogs and so must find breeders who will supply them with their stock. By dealing directly with a breeder one may save time and possibly a little money.

The selection of the individual puppy may depend on a number of factors. Both male and female Lhasa Apsos make good pets. Both can be housebroken by the usual methods. Males are less expensive because they are in greater excess than females. Males are usually born in a two to one ratio to females and this over-supply will keep the price of the males lower. This, however, would not necessarily be the case in the selection of a show dog.

A puppy should not be taken from its dam before it is eight weeks old. It may be weaned by the time it is six weeks of age, but the extra two weeks will give it greater stamina and more confidence when it finally does leave home. This will also give the puppy additional time to adjust to a solid food diet, and the breeder time to have the puppies checked for worms and to have them inoculated.

When there are several puppies to choose from, one has an opportunity to see the personality of each puppy as related to the rest of the litter. Whether a prospective purchaser is intrigued by the most aggressive and outgoing or develops a protective attitude for the most shy and retiring, puppy-play does give a clue to the possible future personality of the dog. Maturity and a new home environment can certainly modify a personality, but usually some of the original traits will still remain.

While watching the puppy romp, the prospective buyer will be able to make sure that the puppy does not limp or have any other obvious physical disability. The puppy should be examined to ascertain that his eyes are clear and that he has no sores or cuts on his body. Once this superficial physical examination has been completed, the buyer has an opportunity to make the other rather subjective decisions such as those relating to color and size.

Lhasa Apsos are seen in just about all colors and combinations of colors, although the preference of many breeders and owners today is still the lion-colored dog. The pet owner may prefer the darker colored dog since it is often less expensive than the bright gold. In many cases, however, a prospective buyer falls in love with a certain puppy and decides to buy that one regardless of other factors to be considered or any predetermined requirements that he might have established. Many dogs are sold to compulsive buyers.

The quantity and texture of hair on the Lhasa Apso is something that should be studied. A puppy that has a very sparse and short coat will probably never have a very heavy one. On the other hand, a puppy with great quantities of dense, soft hair will probably always have a good coat that will require a lot of brushing to keep it free from mats and tangles. The soft coat grows more rapidly but will also require more care. Since many pet owners do not intend to keep up a full coat, quantity and texture may not be important items in the selection of a puppy. An adult dog can always be kept clean and neat by trimming. If his owner does not have the time necessary to keep the full adult coat brushed properly, the dog will be much more comfortable if he is trimmed, although he will lose the typical Lhasa Apso look.

Before leaving on the final trip to purchase a puppy, one should make sufficient preparations for bringing the puppy home. The easiest way to bring him home is to use a cardboard box that has a lid that can be used in case the puppy gets too nervous and tries to jump out. Several layers of newspapers should be placed in the bottom of the box, with a layer of shredded newspapers or an old towel over them to help absorb any "accidents" that might occur during the ride home.

The puppy will usually sit quietly in the box if he is talked to and if someone will pet him and calm him during the drive home. Occasionally a puppy may become excessively excited and try to climb out of the box. If a firm, calming hand is not enough to keep him confined, closing the lid and talking to him through it will at least keep him where he should be during the drive. At a later time, short drives in the car will accustom him to riding and will make trips to the veterinarian or long drives on vacation much more pleasant for both dog and owner.

As soon as the new puppy arrives home, he should be allowed to romp in a fenced exercise area in the yard—provided, of course, that the weather is pleasant—not cold or wet. This will establish from the very first moment the puppy is in his new home that he is to do certain things outside. Returning him to this place frequently and on a fixed schedule will start the housebreaking pattern promptly and should prove to be a most effective method.

One of the first places a young puppy should visit is the veterinarian's office. The puppy will undoubtedly have been given a temporary shot by the kennel owner from whom he was purchased. The temporary shot will be good for a period of about two weeks, and a permanent inoculation can be given when the puppy is three months old. This is extremely important for the health of the puppy and should never be neglected.

There are three common diseases to which dogs are susceptible. They are distemper, hepatitis, and leptospirosis. These diseases are to be considered serious because they are frequently fatal when immunization has been neglected. Even though they are serious diseases, there are effective inoculations against all three. A three-in-one shot can be administered by the veterinarian, followed at a later date by a booster shot. When the puppy is six months old he should also receive immunization against rabies.

While the puppy is at the veterinarian's office, he should have his nails clipped, for long nails cause discomfort to the dog when he walks. The owner should learn to clip the nails himself, for they should be clipped about every ten days, and learning to perform this simple chore can save a great deal of money over a period of time. (See page 38 for instructions on this procedure.)

While at the veterinarian's office, the dog's ears should be checked to make sure that they are free from hair and wax. The dog should also be checked to make certain that he is free from worms and other parasites.

A good veterinarian will keep the dog in good health and assure a life span of twelve to fourteen years for the Lhasa Apso as well as to keep the owner from needless care and worry. The selection of the right veterinarian is a matter that should warrant a good deal of consideration.

When the new owner purchases his puppy he will receive from the breeder a blue registration certificate from The American Kennel Club and a copy of the pedigree. The registration certificate will contain the information required to complete the transfer of ownership from the breeder to the new owner. The paper contains such information as the names of the sire and the dam, the date of whelping, the color and sex of the puppy, and the registration number of the litter.

At the time of purchase the breeder must provide certain information on the reverse side of the registration certificate. This will transfer ownership of the puppy to the new owner. The certificate must be signed by the owner and forwarded to The American Kennel Club along with the necessary fee specified on the certificate.

When filling out the information on the front side of the certificate, the owner will also have an opportunity to name the puppy. Two names must be submitted. The first choice will be accepted unless it has already been used for another dog.

When the certificate is returned by The American Kennel Club, it should be kept in a safe place, for it represents the title of ownership of the dog. Information contained in this document will be needed should the dog ever be entered in competition at a sanctioned show, or should the dog be used for breeding.

RJB George at five months of age shows a typical puppy coat.

Mrs. Jack Slade on a davenport taken over by Maytime Lhasa Apsos.

Ch. Shaggy Wonder Queen of Sheba, a foundation bitch of Stonewall Kennels.

A Saint and a sinner after a hard romp in the fields.

The Adult Lhasa Apso

The American Kennel Club (A.K.C.) recognizes only purebred dogs. It establishes rules for the breeding of these dogs and offers guidance to the breeders.

One of the first things that the A.K.C. does when it recognizes a new breed is to establish a "Standard," or detailed description for that particular breed, which is then used as a measure for evaluating the dogs.

The Standard is a result of the efforts of breeders who have sought the recognition of the A.K.C. for their particular breed. Over a period of years they have maintained careful breeding records of the dogs. They have acted as a semi-official registering agency for all information. This includes litter registration, stud book data, and other information pertinent to the development of the breed—such as records of its history and evolution, and of dogs imported and exported.

After a probationary period in which the consistency of the breed has been demonstrated, The American Kennel Club will allow the breed to be exhibited in the Miscellaneous Class at dog shows. Following a period of time during which the judges have an opportunity to become familiar with the breed and the exhibitors have an opportunity to demonstrate that there is sufficient interest, the breed will be officially recognized and shown in regular breed and Group competition.

At the time of recognition, the Standard of the breed is formally accepted. Judges and breeders use this official description in determining the quality of the dogs. Standards are difficult documents to prepare and to interpret. To the novice in the breed, it will probably be a difficult process to construct a mental picture of a particular breed from the description in the Standard. In some cases one must be familiar with the breed in order to grasp the language of the Standard.

Size and weight descriptions are the easiest to interpret. However, when adjectives appear in abundance it is difficult to determine the exact connotation the writer had in mind. Since interpretations vary from time to time and new breeders become dominant and active in breed clubs through the years, Standards may be rewritten. Such evolutionary changes help to explain why pictures of breed winners of twenty or thirty years ago often appear quite different from those winning today.

The American Kennel Club, in nearly all cases, has recorded the date on which a breed Standard was accepted as the official statement of the breed. The Standard for the Lhasa Apso is the fourth oldest recorded. It is pre-dated only by the Standard for the Great Pyrenees, approved February 13, 1935; the Standard for the Sealyham, approved March 12, 1935; and the Standard for the Scottish Deerhound, approved in March 1935. The Standard for the Rottweiler carries the same date as that of the Lhasa Apso—April 9, 1935.

Trying to visualize the Lhasa Apso from the Standard description is more difficult than with some other breeds because the Lhasa Apso Standard is so brief. Newly revised Standards for other breeds are longer and more detailed, which does seem to help in visualizing the breed but also creates some other problems in breeding programs because of the specificity of the wording.

A good exercise for both the new fancier and the experienced breeder is to sit ringside at a show with the Standard in hand and measure those dogs in the ring against it. If, after the judging, the spectator has an opportunity to go over the winning dogs, he can learn a good deal more than by the ringside study alone.

Character—Gay and assertive, but chary of strangers.

Size—Variable, but about 10 inches or 11 inches at shoulder for dogs, bitches slightly smaller.

Color—Golden, sandy, honey, dark grizzle, slate, smoke, parti-color, black, white or brown. This being the true Tibetan Lion-dog, golden or lionlike colors are preferred. Other colors in order as above. Dark tips to ears and beard are an asset.

Body Shape—The length from point of shoulders to point of buttocks longer than height at withers, well ribbed up, strong loin, well-developed quarters and thighs.

Coat—Heavy, straight, hard, not woolly nor silky, of good length, and very dense.

Mouth and Muzzle—Mouth level, otherwise slightly undershot preferable. Muzzle of medium length; a square muzzle is objectionable.

Head—Heavy head furnishings with good fall over eyes, good whiskers and beard; skull narrow, falling away behind the eyes in a marked degree, not quite flat, but not domed or apple-shaped; straight foreface of fair length. Nose black, about 1½ inches long, or the length from the tip of nose to eye to be roughly about one-third of the total length from nose to back of skull.

Eyes—Dark brown, neither very large and full, nor very small and sunk.

Ears—Pendant, heavily feathered.

Legs—Forelegs straight; both forelegs and hind legs heavily furnished with hair.

Feet—Well feathered, should be round and catlike, with good pads.

Tail and Carriage—Well feathered, should be carried well over back in a screw; there may be a kink at the end. A low carriage of stern is a serious fault.

Approved April 9, 1935

The Standard for any breed is of greatest help to those who have raised dogs for some time, for they know what some of the less obvious terminology means. Interpretation of some of the phraseology is often difficult for the novice in the breed. Perhaps the easiest way to facilitate interpretation of the Standard is to clarify those statements which need to be expanded.

The size of the Lhasa Apsos being shown today has increased slightly over those shown ten and fifteen years ago. The larger dogs are winning, and as a result breeders are gradually increasing the size of the stock that they are breeding. Many serious breeders believe that a larger dog makes a better picture in the Group ring and is a better representative of the breed. The larger ones appear to move more soundly and have increased stamina. The twelve to fourteen pound winners of the 1950s and early 1960s would look like puppies beside the eighteen to twenty-two pound dogs seen in the ring today.

Some breeders have, moreover, made conscientious efforts to increase the size of the Lhasa Apso in order to draw a clearly defined line between the Lhasa Apso and the Shih Tzu. The confusion between the two breeds has always been great and probably will continue to be so, but an obvious size difference would eliminate some of the difficulty. There is, however, a tendency for the Shih Tzu to increase in size also.

One of the outstanding features of the Lhasa Apso is his magnificent coat. While the coat is a thing of beauty, it is also an object for concern because it requires great care if it is to mature properly and to remain in good condition.

The coat should be heavy, very dense, and of good length. In the show ring, most Lhasa Apsos past one year of age carry a coat that reaches to the floor. On occasion, even younger dogs are seen with the same abundant coat. The coat is one indication of the overall condition of the dog, for he will not produce the elegant coat if he is not in proper weight and in good health. When the coat condition is poor, it is frequently an indication of an improperly balanced diet or of poor health in general. A heavy, dense coat means that one cannot see through it where it touches the floor. On occasion, however, a coat will reach the floor but be so thin that it is possible to see under the dog. This is usually caused by poor grooming with the resultant loss of undercoat.

The Lhasa Apso in good coat carries a quantity of undercoat which is in proportion to the texture of the outer coat. Three types of coats are seen in the Lhasa Apso today—hard, woolly, and silky. The Standard mentions all three and indicates that the last two are not acceptable. The correct texture is hard and the hair should be straight. Fortunately, of the three possible types, the hard coat is by far the easiest to care for. The woolly coat is a fast maturing coat which is extremely dense and reaches great length—usually to the floor—well before the dog is a year of age. The woolly coat is the most difficult to care for since it requires daily or even, on occasion, twice daily brushings. The undercoat on this type of dog is also extremely dense, which further complicates grooming.

The silky coat is less difficult to care for than the woolly one, but, again, it is not the correct texture. It is a coat more suited to certain Toy breeds and really is out of place on a dog the size of the Lhasa Apso. The undercoat is moderate when the hair is silky.

The correct texture is hard—even stiff—hair which will hang straight to the floor without any tendency to curl or wave. It is a coat which matures more slowly than the other two but is by far the easiest to groom. While some dogs with the hard coat require grooming only once a week, best results are obtained by more frequent grooming sessions—usually two or three per week. With the hard coat, the undercoat is well balanced in proportion to the outer coat. It serves to give body to the coat and is a vestige of the days when the dog lived in the high cold mountains of Tibet and needed this texture and quantity of hair for protection for the severe weather.

It would seem wise to include in a breeding program only those dogs with the correct coat. The situation is complicated, however, by the fact that on occasion more than one type of coat will appear in the same litter. The woolly coated dog matures more rapidly, not only in coat but also in body, and usually develops a greater rib spring. It therefore becomes a question of using this type in a breeding program occasionally to improve the body balance.

The Standard indicates that the Lhasa Apso is to be gay and assertive but that he should also be chary of strangers. This describes quite adequately the personality and temperament of the Lhasa Apso as he is seen as the family pet at home. He will be chary of strangers, but he is not an aggressive dog nor does he have any tendency toward viciousness.

As shown in the ring today, and in the way in which the judge sees and evaluates the dog, the Lhasa Apso is really more regal and aloof than chary. Only rarely do we see a Lhasa Apso with a tail wagging happily while in the ring. With the exception of puppies or novice dogs, very seldom do we see one pull back or shy from examination. The personality description of the Standard is, therefore, only partially true and would not be of great service to the ringside observer, for these traits just do not appear there. The description is perhaps more suited to the Lhasa Apso while he is romping at home.

The Lhasa Apso is a breed of average or above average intelligence. While only a very limited number have been taken through to their obedience titles, this is certainly not an indication of lack of trainability on the part of the dogs, but rather a lack of interest or perseverance on the part of the owners.

The Lhasa Apso will learn the routine of a new home readily and will adapt to it. He will train himself to do those things which give pleasure to his new owner. He is also sly enough to learn most rapidly those things which bring him a reward in the form of some special treat or a dog biscuit. He is, in reality, extremely bright when he wants to be, but he can be somewhat bull-headed when his interest has not been sufficiently whetted to undertake some specific task.

Certain characteristics are considered undesirable in the Lhasa Apso, and a prospective purchaser should avoid selecting a puppy showing such characteristics. Should these traits not appear in the puppy but develop later, that particular dog or bitch should not be included in a breeding program. This will help preserve the integrity of the strain.

Eyes that are excessively prominent give cause for concern. Eye injuries are common with this type eye for there is not sufficient protection, and a minor injury can turn into a permanently scarred eye that ulcerates or becomes milky.

A dog with an excessively undershot mouth or one that is overshot at all should be avoided. These are inherited qualities and will be passed on to the offspring. In Lhasa Apsos today there is greater uniformity of mouths, and teeth are, as a rule, straight and evenly aligned. There are, of course, exceptions, but conscientious breeding programs on the part of serious breeders have brought about great improvement of bite.

The fact that the Standard for the breed is so old in comparison with those of other breeds indicates that breeders have endeavored to conform to the original type of Lhasa Apso. The Standard, however, should be examined regularly to determine that one's breeding program actually produces the correct results. Breeding and showing to the Standard is a goal to be sought by all breeders.

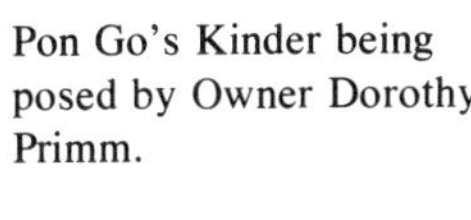

Pandan Ani-Coci posed by her owner, Mary Anne Stafford.

Pon Go's Kinder being posed by Owner Dorothy Primm.

A Lhasa Apso in a pet trim may not be an object of glory, but he is comfortable and a happy house pet.

Eight-week-old RJB Bartholomew shows the happy alertness of the Lhasa Apso.

RJB Irwin hams it up for the camera. The parti-color makes a striking appearance.

Personality of the Lhasa Apso

The Lhasa Apso is a dog of charm and grace. He is a royal dog of royal ancestry, and he knows it. At times he demonstrates an aloofness that can almost border on disdain. He is a true reflection of his pampered background.

The original practice of selective inbreeding carried out by the tenders of the royal dogs in the lamaseries of Tibet has deeply etched its genetic pattern on the modern dog. Current breeding programs are breeding out some of the less desirable personality traits, and may well do so.

One of the unusual traits of the Lhasa Apso in the past was his tendency to be excessively chary of strangers. This reticence led to some problems in the show ring in the past since the judge was the stranger, and a friendship was not likely to develop easily. There have been magnificent specimens of dogs in the past that would have gone Best in Show if they could have been examined in their own back yards. Extreme chariness is one of the least desirable qualities and is being bred out of the strain.

The cult of the personality is manifesting itself as one of the major goals of breeding programs. Lhasa Apso owners of long standing have grown accustomed to the breed's chariness and do not find it particularly annoying. It does, however, present somewhat of a problem when trying to sell a dog to someone not accustomed to the breed.

The size of the Lhasa Apso, as first exhibited in the United States, has decreased considerably from those dogs originally owned by the Dalai Lama. The first show specimens were in the ten to fifteen pound range, with some being even smaller. In the last few years, however, size and substance have increased greatly. There are a couple of possible reasons for this change. One is that a conscientious effort has been made to differentiate between the Lhasa Apso in the Non-Sporting Group and the smaller, heavy-coated dogs in the Toy Group. A Non-Sporting dog should present a different picture from a Toy lap dog. A second possible explanation is that the larger dog tends to be a stronger dog and his size makes him a better contender in the Group. He will, therefore, not be overlooked and left unnoticed at the end of the Group line.

The Lhasa Apso that is a house pet is the self-appointed guardian of the house and the inspector of all comings and goings. He announces all visitors with the usual—or even unusual—amount of barking to alert all that an invasion is about to take place and that sufficient preparations should be made. The barking will, of course, be accompanied by the normal amount of sniffing, advancing, and retreating before peace returns.

The Lhasa Apso, more than many breeds, seems to attach himself either to men or women and tends to ignore whichever sex is not his favorite. In homes where there are many children he may even help in underscoring the generation gap by aligning himself with either the youngsters or with the adults.

He makes himself content on the furniture, the floor, the front seat of the car, or just about anywhere so long as he can be near the one individual in the family that he has singled out as his special friend. He maintains this loyalty tenaciously in spite of bribes and enticements from others, for loyalty is one of his outstanding characteristics. He learns the living pattern of a new home quickly and can adapt to it easily.

The Lhasa Apso does make a good family pet. He is small enough to be cuddly for the youngsters, but still large enough to be substantial and less fragile than a Toy dog. The Lhasa Apso is low enough to the ground to make grabbing a leg less inviting than in the case of a taller dog. The Lhasa Apso is a loving dog with an even temperament. He romps good-naturedly with the youngsters but also will be willing to rest and lie quietly when they do. His occasional bursts of energy as he runs frantically around the back yard are a delight to his master.

The coat of the pet-quality Lhasa Apso should be kept clean and neat. The owners might, therefore, want to keep it clipped shorter than it normally grows. If this is the easiest and most convenient way for the family, and the most comfortable for the dog, the decision to clip him should not be a difficult one. The dog will be a little uncomfortable the first day or two after he has been trimmed. The new trim must also be a little embarrassing for him, for he will occasionally hide or stay very close to his favorite master until he adjusts to his new appearance.

The adaptability of the Lhasa Apso is one of his strong qualities and one that makes him a good family pet. He does adjust easily and is willing to accept new challenges, new adventures, and new surroundings without becoming upset.

Most Lhasa Apsos love to be pampered and to be fussed over. They will respond in kind to loving treatment and special attention. They do enjoy sitting on an owner's lap, but being heavy-coated dogs, they get warm very soon and will look for a cooler place, usually on the tile floor or in a doorway where there might be a slight breeze. During the warm months they may just decide to pass up the opportunity for lap-sitting. To help them keep cool, plenty of clean, fresh water should always be available.

The Lhasa Apso is not only a good companion for the family but also a friend and protector of other dogs. One of my old champion bitches who is top dog in the house put herself in charge of a Yorkshire Terrier puppy that had sprained her leg while playing. The bitch mothered the puppy and kept all the other dogs away until the leg healed. This friendship has continued on both sides through the years, with the Lhasa Apso still mothering the aging Yorkshire.

If Lhasa Apsos were people, many would probably be in the movies or on the stage, for they are truly "hams" at heart. They discover very quickly which of their antics bring pleasure and they repeat them with a strong-willed determination. One young puppy learned that he received great praise and dog biscuits for having taught himself to sit and beg. When company arrives he jumps up on a footstool and sits up until he is properly recognized.

A neighbor had a Lhasa Apso who had been taught to shake hands. He enjoyed performing this trick many times each day without even being asked to do so. One evening the neighbor's house caught fire, bringing the fire trucks and dozens of spectators. The Lhasa Apso became the self-appointed host, going from person to person shaking hands. He seemed most determined not to miss anyone in his capacity as official greeter. Neither the noise nor the confusion seemed to deter him in his task.

Every Lhasa Apso owner has a storehouse of stories he would be glad to share with any willing listener—and he may even try to share them with a few unwilling listeners.

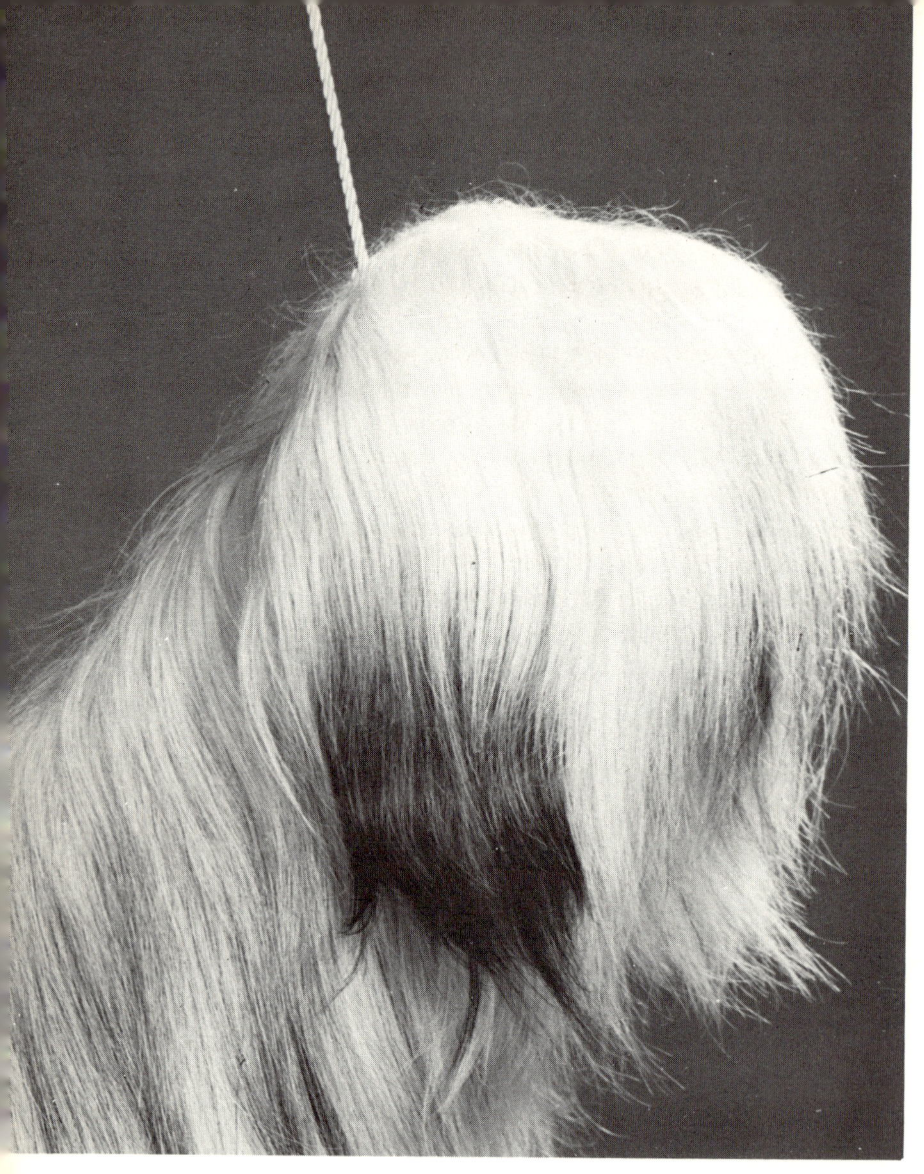

A head study of American and Canadian Ch. Caprice's Tsan Tse, showing how the Lhasa Apso head was groomed in the past to cover the eyes completely.

Preparing the Lhasa Apso for Show

The conditioning of the Lhasa Apso is of prime importance both for his health and for his happiness. The key to proper conditioning is proper diet, so a well-balanced diet should be maintained at all times. Meals can be varied to make them interesting without sacrificing standards of nutrition, and vitamin and mineral supplements can be added.

During the past few years much money has been spent in the study of animal nutrition, especially that of the dog. Research in animal nutrition is, in fact, much farther advanced than is that of man. There are a number of nutritionists in the schools of veterinary medicine who are working with commercial concerns that produce food for animals, and practically none working with the major universities doing research on nutrition for humans.

In addition to a well-balanced diet, proper exercise is necessary for all dogs. An hour or two each day should be set aside to exercise the dog. This can be accomplished by the dog's being allowed to romp in a fenced area, or by his being taken for a walk. A well-drained run covered with three or four inches of gravel is easy to keep clean and will keep the dog out of the mud on rainy days. An occasional lime treatment eliminates odors. Dry lime can be sprinkled over the surface of the run and then washed through thoroughly with a hose to prevent the dog's picking up the lime on the pads of his feet.

A clean exercise area helps keep the dog clean and eliminates the need for unnecessarily frequent bathing. Bathing does not hurt the dog's coat or health providing it is done with care. Show dogs are usually bathed once a week, and they are able to grow beautiful coats.

There are a number of good shampoos prepared especially for dogs. In addition, liquid non-detergent soaps may be used. They are effective and are usually much less expensive. Cream rinses can be applied to help keep down matting after bathing. All grooming products should be used with caution the first few times to determine the reaction of a particular dog. The owner can save a great deal of time when drying the dog is he uses an electric hair dryer.

The coat of the Lhasa Apso is one of its outstanding characteristics and the one that attracts the attention and interest of dog admirers everywhere. A Lhasa Apso with a neat, full coat is truly a remarkable example of the breed, while, in contrast, one whose coat has not been cared for is not only unattractive but also unsuccessful in the show ring.

Proper nutrition is necessary for a healthy coat. A dog cannot grow a proper coat unless he is fed a well-balanced diet. Before he can produce the quantity of coat he should have, he must have gained and must maintain the weight consistent with his size.

A regular schedule of bathing and grooming should be established early in the puppy's life so that the owner is always well ahead of any coat problem that might arise. Brushing should be started while the puppy is only a few weeks old. His coat will need very little real attention at this early age, but the brushing will help train the dog for some of the longer grooming sessions which will follow at a later date. The easiest way to start training is to brush the puppy's coat gently while holding him in your lap.

Sometime between the age of eight and ten months a puppy will begin to lose his first coat. As the old hair falls out it will become matted in the new coat. Daily brushings will be required for about a month until all the puppy coat has been shed.

A clean coat is a healthy coat. A coat that is allowed to become

A black Lhasa Apso is striking but does not win with the regularity of the goldens.

dirty will tangle quickly and develop small mats which will either break the hair or cause it to be broken in working out the mat. If the coat is dirty or sticky or caked with mud—which is often the case when the dog is allowed to run freely in the yard—the dog should be bathed thoroughly before attempting to brush him. A partial bath or even a partial rinsing can save needless work and worry.

With the proper training, the adult dog should lie still on his side so that he can be groomed easily and the groomer can use both hands in working on the stomach and under the legs where mats can develop rather quickly. Since the Lhasa Apso has the double coat, care must be taken to groom from the skin out. Many inexperienced groomers do not get the tiny mats out next to the skin, and this not only destroys the undercoat but frequently causes the outer coat to become entangled in it.

With the dog lying on its side, the groomer should begin under the muzzle, pushing the hair back. Then gradually, layer by layer, he should brush the hair towards himself, using a large stainless steel pin brush. Large mats can be detected easily, but small mats are felt only by the pulling pressure on the brush. When these are encountered, one should work the mat out with the fingers or with a single tooth of a comb, pulling one hair loose at a time if necessary in order to avoid breaking the hairs.

When the groomer has covered a small section with the pin brush, he should go back over the same area with the slicker brush; but this should be done very carefully, for the slicker brush will cut the hair if used improperly. By using the slicker brush, one will discover new and even smaller mats, since the teeth of the slicker brush are set closer together. Again, these mats should be worked out carefully. The final step is to go over the same area a third time with a metal comb. This last step is important, for by the time the comb goes smoothly through the hair, the groomer can be sure that there are no mats left.

After completing the area under the muzzle, the groomer should move to the chest, the underside of the leg, and then to the outer side of the leg. After brushing the stomach and underside of the dog and both sides of the rear leg, the groomer should turn the dog onto its stomach and repeat the brushing process again, moving

Ch. Glenn's Pines Nanda
Devi, showing a typical
coat for a ten-month-old
puppy.

A well-drained exercise
yard is a necessity for
raising puppies.

from the head to the rear and brushing up to the part. With the dog still on its stomach, the tail can be brushed easily before turning the dog onto its other side and repeating the whole process again.

After grooming the dog a few times, the groomer will discover the ease of the technique, and, with practice, the length of time required to brush the dog thoroughly and carefully will diminish. The regularity of the brushing is of great importance in keeping the Lhasa Apso ready for the ring. With a definite grooming schedule, mats seldom develop and the dog will produce a coat of even length with healthy hair ends.

While grooming the dog, the groomer should use a little hair conditioner or water spray, which helps to cleanse foreign matter from hair ends and to prevent damage. There are any number of hair conditioners available through pet shops or at drug stores. Certain coats react adversely to given conditioners; it is, therefore, wise to experiment early on the puppy coat or on the underside of the dog in order to find the spray most successful for the particular texture of coat.

While a part in the hair down the middle of the back of the dog is natural since hair that length has to fall to one side or the other, a straight line part is something that must be made by the groomer. The easiest way to get an even part after the dog is completely brushed is to use a knitting needle. Starting at the head and moving toward the tail, the groomer can part a two or three inch section at a time, sliding the needle down the backbone and then slowly drawing it up to allow the hair to fall to either side. When it is finished and straight, the entire length of the part should be sprayed in order to hold it in place.

Following the techniques and steps described above may be too time-consuming for the average pet owner. In this case it is kinder to the dog to keep its hair trimmed short, especially behind the ears and on the inside of the legs. He will not look like a show Lhasa Apso, but clipping the coat will eliminate the possibility of the hair's becoming so matted that it tears the skin and causes an infection. A summer clip, similar to the puppy clip in Poodles, is seen more and more frequently nowadays. Clipping seems to be a good compromise for those who love the Lhasa Apso personality but are not willing to groom a full show coat.

Showing is a combination of fun and hard work. The pleasure comes from meeting other breeders and exhibitors at the show and in being in competition with them in the show ring. Being able to see one's breeding line in comparison to those of others is also an educational opportunity. The owner not only receives a professional opinion from the judge but also learns to evaluate his own dog as he watches other dogs parade in the ring. The judge has the advantage of putting his hands on all the dogs in competition. Going over each dog is an extremely important part of the judging of long-haired breeds, for a beautiful long coat can cover numerous imperfections.

Getting the Lhasa Apso ready for the ring on the day of the show follows the bathing and the preliminary grooming the exhibitor did before leaving for the show circuit. The coat must be groomed meticulously from the skin out so that there are no skin mats which will destroy the natural outline of the dog. By the time a dog is old enough to be shown in the ring, he should have been thoroughly trained to lie on his side for whatever period of time is necessary to groom him completely. This training should be started months in advance so that the dog will not have to be disciplined the day of the show. The handler should avoid those actions which might make the dog nervous before he goes into the ring.

On the day of the show, the handler should groom the right side of the dog first, saving the "show side" for last. After each layer of brushing, the coat should be sprayed lightly with water or a diluted coat-dressing to help keep the hair from flying and to keep it straight and in place for the succeeding layers.

After the dog has been brushed completely, he should be set up on the grooming table for the final treatment of the part. After completing the body part, the groomer should return to the head to make the horizontal part from eye to eye which separates the hair that will be brushed down into the chin whiskers and that which will be brushed upward and back over the head. Rubbing a little coat dressing into the hair above the eyes will keep the hair parted while the dog is in the ring. Some years ago the hair was brushed completely over the eyes, with only the nose to tail part permissible. This practice, however, made it difficult for the judge to examine the eyes without disturbing the head coat completely.

When the class is called, the handler should already have determined where his dog will show to the best advantage, and he should try to get in that place in line if he can accomplish it tactfully. If the dog gaits rapidly, the head of the line would be the preferred position. If the dog moves slowly, however, the end of the line is the obvious choice. A slow moving dog in the middle of the line only calls attention to the fact that the dog does not move well. The end of the line is also the best place to show the dog that keeps looking back at the dog following him. The handler should take advantage of those techniques which will show his dog to its best advantage. It should be remembered, however, that a competent judge will find the best dog no matter where he is in line, so long as he is shown to advantage.

In the ring the dog should be set up and then worked just enough to keep him in pose. Over-handling of a dog tends to make him nervous and prevents the judge from getting a good look at him. The handler should remember that a judge is always looking at his dog. Even if a judge is at the other end of the line, he may glance back to see how your dog looks in comparison to the one he is examining. Allowing a dog to sit or sag can lose a placement.

Obviously, there is no perfect dog, for every dog has strong points and weak points. Consequently, the strong points should be emphasized and the weak ones minimized. This is not unethical, for it must be remembered that all exhibitors have the same set of difficulties. The judge will pick the best dog in the class, so the exhibitor must prove to him that his dog has more strong qualities than the other dogs in the ring. The judge will select the best one present that particular day in comparison with the other entries.

After the judge has examined the individual dog (usually on the table for the Lhasa Apso), the coat will again have to be straightened out. A few swipes with a fine-toothed comb will accomplish this, especially if the pre-ring grooming has been done correctly. This extra combing will show the dog at his best on the individual go-round.

A head study of Ch. Luty Tony of Darno.

Grooming and
General Coat Care

Although coat types, textures, and patterns may seem purely arbitrary matters of little consequence, they are among the important characteristics that distinguish one breed from another. Actually, each breed has been developed to serve a specific purpose, and the coat that is considered typical for the breed is also the one most appropriate for the dog's specialized use—be it as guard, hunting companion, herder, or pet. A knowledge of the breed Standard approved by The American Kennel Club is helpful to the owner who takes pride in owning a well-groomed dog, typical of its breed.

Dogs with short, smooth coats (such as the Weimaraner, Basset, Beagle, smooth Dachshund and Chihuahua) usually shed only moderately and their coats require little routine grooming other than thorough brushing with a bristle brush or hound glove. For exhibition in the show ring, the whiskers, or "feelers," are trimmed close to the muzzle, but no other trimming is needed.

The wire coat of the Airedale, Wire Fox Terrier, Miniature Schnauzer, or Wirehaired Dachshund should be stripped or plucked in show trim at regular intervals. The dog can then be kept well groomed by thorough combing and brushing.

Curly coated breeds such as the Curly Coated Retriever, and the American and Irish Water Spaniels, generally require no special coat care other than frequent brushing. True curly coated breeds are very curly indeed and are not to be confused with breeds such as the Golden Retriever, Gordon Setter, Brittany Spaniel, and English Springer Spaniel, which have slightly curled or wavy coats of somewhat silky texture. The longer hair, or "feathers," typically found on tail, legs, ears, and chest of these breeds should be trimmed slightly to make the outline neater.

(UPPER LEFT) Wire brush (RIGHT) Bristle brush
(LOWER LEFT) Comb—Hound glove.

They are not "trimmed to pattern," however, as are such long-haired breeds as the Kerry Blue Terrier and the Poodle, which, when shown in the breed ring, must be clipped and trimmed in the patterns specified in the breed Standards.

The Longhaired Dachshund, the Borzoi, and the Yorkshire Terrier have long but comparatively silky coats, whereas the Newfoundland and the Rough Collie have long straight coats with rather harsh texture. Long coats must be kept brushed out thoroughly to eliminate mats and snarls.

The dog should be taught from puppyhood that a grooming session is a time for business, not for play. He should be handled gently, though, for it is essential to avoid hurting him in any way. Grooming time should be pleasant for both dog and master.

Tools required vary with the breed, but always include combs, brushes, and nail clippers and files. Combs should have wide-spaced teeth with rounded ends so that the dog's skin will not be scratched accidentally. For the same reason, brushes with natural bristles are usually preferable to those with synthetic bristles that may be too fine and sharp.

A light, airy, pleasant place in which to work is desirable, and it is of the utmost importance that neither dog nor master be distracted by other dogs, cats, or people. Consequently, it is usually preferable that grooming be done indoors.

Particularly for large or medium breeds, a sturdy grooming table is desirable. Many owners hold small puppies or Toy dogs during grooming sessions, athough it is better if they, too, are groomed on a table. Large and medium size dogs should be taught to jump onto the table and to jump off again when grooming is completed. Small dogs must be lifted on and off to avoid falls and possible injury. The dog should stand while the back and upper portions of the body are groomed, and lie on his side while underparts of his body are brushed, nails clipped, etc.

Before each session, the dog should be permitted to relieve himself. Once grooming is begun, it is important to avoid keeping the dog standing so long that he becomes tired. If a good deal of grooming is needed, it should be done in two or more short periods.

It is almost impossible to brush too much, and show dogs are often brushed for a full half hour a day, year round. If you cannot brush your dog every day, you should brush him a minimum of two or three times a week. Brushing removes loose skin particles and stimulates circulation, thereby improving condition of the skin. It also stimulates secretion of the natural skin oils that make the coat look healthy and beautiful.

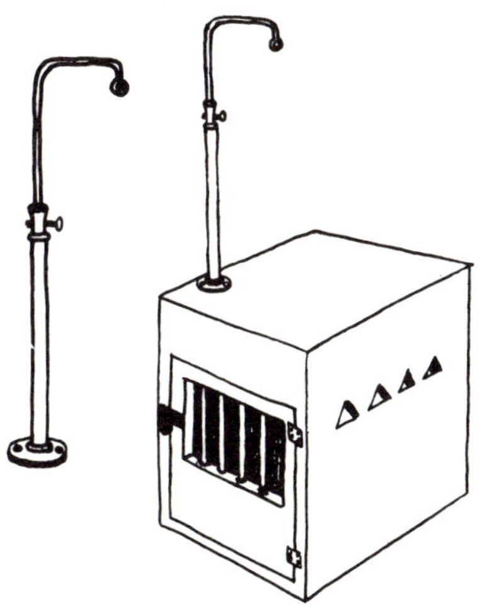

Dog crate with grooming—table top is ideal—providing rigid, well supported surface on which to groom dog, and serving as indoor kennel for puppy or grown dog. Rubber matting provides non-slip surface. Dog's collar may be attached to adjustable arm. Lightweight and readily transported yet sturdy, the crate is especially useful to owner who takes dog with him when he travels.

Before brushing, any burs adhering to the coat, as well as matted hair, should be carefully removed, using the fingers and coarse toothed comb with a gentle, teasing motion to avoid tearing the coat. The coat should first be brushed lightly in the direction in which the hair grows. Next, it should be brushed vigorously in the opposite direction, a small portion at a time, making sure the bristles penetrate the hair to the skin, until the entire coat has been brushed thoroughly and all loose soil removed. Then the coat should be brushed in the direction the hair grows, until every hair is sleekly in place.

The dog that is kept well brushed needs bathing only rarely. Once or twice a year is usually enough. Except for unusual circumstances when his coat becomes excessively soiled, no puppy under six months of age should be bathed in water. If it is necessary to bathe a puppy, extreme care must be exercised so that he will not become chilled. No dog should be bathed during cold weather and then permitted to go outside immediately. Whatever the weather, the dog should always be given a good run outdoors and permitted to relieve himself before he is bathed.

Various types of "dry baths" are available at pet supply stores. In general, they are quite satisfactory when circumstances are such that a bath in water is impractical. Dry shampoos are usually rubbed into the dog's coat thoroughly, then removed by vigorous towelling or brushing.

Before starting a water bath, the necessary equipment should be assembled. This includes a tub of appropriate size, and another tub or pail for rinse water. (A small hose with a spray nozzle—one that may be attached to the water faucet—is ideal for rinsing the dog.) A metal or plastic cup for dipping water, special dog shampoo, a small bottle of mineral or olive oil, and a supply of absorbent cotton should be placed nearby, as well as a supply of heavy towels, a wash cloth, and the dog's combs and brushes.

The amount of water required will vary according to the size of the dog, but should reach no higher than the dog's elbows. Bath water and rinse water should be slightly warmer than lukewarm, but should not be hot.

To avoid accidentally getting water in the dog's ears, place a small amount of absorbent cotton in each. With the dog standing in the tub, wet his body by using the cup to pour water over him. Take care to avoid wetting the head, and be careful to avoid getting water or shampoo in the eyes. (If you should accidentally do so, placing a few drops of mineral or olive oil in the inner corner of the eye will bring relief.) When the dog is thoroughly wet, put a small amount of shampoo on his back and work up a lather, rubbing briskly. Wash his entire body and then rinse as much of the shampoo as possible from the coat by dipping water from the tub and pouring it over the dog.

Dip the wash cloth into clean water, wring it out enough so it won't drip, then wash the dog's head, taking care to avoid the eyes. Remove the cotton from the dog's ears and sponge them gently, inside and out. Shampoo should never be used inside the ears, so if they are extremely soiled, sponge them clean with cotton saturated with mineral or olive oil. (Between baths, the ears should be cleaned frequently in the same way.)

Replace the cotton in the ears, then use the cup and container of rinse water (or hose and spray nozzle) to rinse the dog thoroughly. Quickly wrap a towel around him, remove him from the tub, and towel him as dry as possible. To avoid getting an impromptu bath yourself, you must act quickly, for once he is out of the tub, the dog will instinctively shake himself.

While the hair is still slightly damp, use a clean comb or brush to remove any tangles. If the hair is allowed to dry first, it may be completely impossible to remove them.

So far as routine grooming is concerned, the dog's eyes require little attention. Some dogs have a slight accumulation of mucus in the corner of the eyes upon waking mornings. A salt solution (1 teaspoon of table salt to one pint of warm, sterile water) can be sponged around the eyes to remove the stain. During grooming sessions it is well to inspect the eyes, since many breeds are prone to eye injury. Eye problems of a minor nature may be treated at home (see page 50), but it is imperative that any serious eye abnormality be called to the attention of the veterinarian immediately.

Feeding hard dog biscuits and hard bones helps to keep tooth surfaces clean. Slight discoloration may be readily removed by rubbing with a damp cloth dipped in salt or baking soda. The dog's head should be held firmly, the lips pulled apart gently, and the teeth rubbed lightly with the dampened cloth. Regular

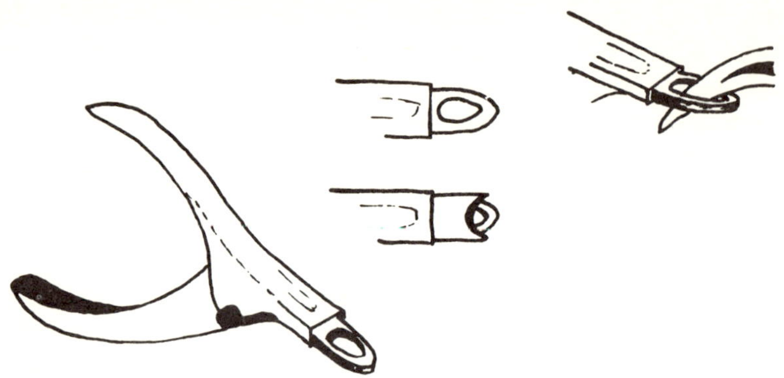

Nail trimmer—center detail shows blade cutting action. Right shows manner of inserting nail in cutter.

care usually keeps the teeth in good condition, but if tartar accumulates, it should be removed by a veterinarian.

If the dog doesn't keep his nails worn down through regular exercise on hard surfaces, they must be trimmed at intervals, for nails that are too long may cause the foot to spread and thus spoil the dog's gait. Neglected nails may even grow so long that they will grow into a circle and puncture the dog's skin. Nails can be cut easily with a nail trimmer that slides over the nail end. The cut is made just outside the faintly pink bloodline that can be seen on white nails. In pigmented nails, the bloodline is not easily seen, so the cut should be made just outside the hooklike projection on the underside of the nails. A few downward strokes with a nail file will smooth the cut surface, and, once shortened, nails can be kept short by filing at regular intervals.

Care must be taken that nails are not cut too short, since blood vessels may be accidentally severed. Should you accidentally cut a nail so short that it bleeds, apply a mild antiseptic and keep the dog quiet until bleeding stops. Usually, only a few drops of blood will be lost. But once a dog's nails have been cut painfully short, he will usually object when his feet are handled.

The main food elements required by dogs are proteins, fats, and carbohydrates. Vitamins A, B complex, D, and E are essential, as are ample amounts of calcium and iron. Nine other minerals are required in small amounts but are amply provided in almost any diet, so there is no need to be concerned about them.

The most important nutrient is protein and it must be provided every day of the dog's life, for it is essential for normal daily growth and replacement of body tissues burned up in daily activity. Preferred animal protein products are beef, mutton, horse meat, and boned fish. Visceral organs—heart, liver, and tripe— are good but if used in too large quantities may cause diarrhea (bones in large amounts have the same effect). Pork, particularly fat pork, is undesirable. The "meat meal" used in some commercial foods is made from scrap meat processed at high temperatures and then dried. It is not quite so nutritious as fresh meat, but in combination with other protein products, it is an acceptable ingredient in the dog's diet.

Cooked eggs and raw egg yolk are good sources of protein, but raw egg white should never be fed since it cannot be digested by the dog and may cause diarrhea. Cottage cheese and milk (fresh, dried, and canned) are high in protein, also. Puppies thrive on milk and it can well be included in the diet of older dogs, too, if mixed with meat, vegetables, and meal. Soy-bean meal, wheat germ meal, and dried brewers yeast are vegetable products high in protein and may be used to advantage in the diet.

Vegetable and animal fats in moderate amounts should be used, especially if a main ingredient of the diet is dry or kibbled food. Fats should not be used excessively or the dog may become overweight. Generally, fats should be increased slightly in the winter and reduced somewhat during warm weather.

Carbohydrates are required for proper assimilation of fats. Dog biscuits, kibble, dog meal, and other dehydrated foods are good sources of carbohydrates, as are cereal products derived from rice, corn, wheat, and ground or rolled oats.

Vegetables supply additional proteins, vitamins, and minerals, and by providing bulk are of value in overcoming constipation. Raw or cooked carrots, celery, lettuce, beets, asparagus, tomatoes, and cooked spinach may be used. They should always be chopped or ground well and mixed with the other food. Various combinations may be used, but a good home-mixed ration for the mature dog consists of two parts of meat and one each of vegetables and dog meal (or cereal product).

Dicalcium phosphate and cod-liver oil are added to puppy diets to ensure inclusion of adequate amounts of calcium and Vitamins A and D. Indiscriminate use of dietary supplements is not only unjustified but may actually be harmful and many breeders feel that their over-use in diets of extremely small breeds may lead to excessive growth as well as to overweight at maturity.

Foods manufactured by well-known and reputable food processors are nutritionally sound and are offered in sufficient variety of flavors, textures, and consistencies that most dogs will find them tempting and satisfying. Canned foods are usually "ready to eat," while dehydrated foods in the form of kibble, meal, or biscuits may require the addition of water or milk. Dried foods containing fat sometimes become rancid, so to avoid an unpalatable change in flavor, the manufacturer may not include fat in dried food but recommend its addition at the time the water or milk is added.

Candy and other sweets are taboo, for the dog has no nutritional need for them and if he is permitted to eat them, he will usually eat less of foods he requires. Also taboo are fried foods, highly seasoned foods and extremely starchy foods, for the dog's digestive tract is not equipped to handle them.

Frozen foods should be thawed completely and warmed at least to lukewarm, while hot foods should be cooled to lukewarm. Food should be in a fairly firm state, for sloppy food is difficult for the dog to digest.

Whether meat is raw or cooked makes little difference, so long as the dog is also given the juice that seeps from the meat during cooking. Bones provide little nourishment, although gnawing bones helps make the teeth strong and helps to keep tartar from accumulating on them. Beef bones, especially large knuckle bones, are best. Fish, poultry, and chop bones should never be given to dogs since they have a tendency to splinter and may puncture the dog's digestive tract.

Clean, fresh, cool water is essential to all dogs and an adequate supply should be readily available twenty-four hours a day from the time the puppy is big enough to walk. Especially during hot weather, the drinking pan should be emptied and refilled at frequent intervals.

Puppies usually are weaned by the time they are six weeks old, so when you acquire a new puppy ten to twelve weeks old, he will already have been started on a feeding schedule. The breeder should supply exact details as to number of meals per day, types and amounts of food offered, etc. It is essential to adhere to this established routine, for drastic changes in diet may produce intestinal upsets.

Until a puppy is six months old, milk formula is an integral part of the diet. A day's supply should be made up at one time and stored in the refrigerator, and the quantity needed for each meal warmed at feeding time. The following combination is good for all breeds:

1 pint whole fresh milk	1 tablespoon lime water
1 raw egg yolk, slightly beaten	1 tablespoon lactose

The two latter items (as well as cod-liver oil and dicalcium phosphate to be added to solid food) are readily available at pet supply stores and drug stores.

At twelve weeks of age the amount of formula given at each feeding will vary from three to four tablespoonfuls for the Toy breeds, to perhaps two cupfuls for the large breeds. If the puppy is on the five-meal-a-day schedule when he leaves the kennel, three of the meals (first, third, and fifth each day) should consist of formula only. On a four-meal schedule, the first and fourth meals should be formula.

In either case, the second meal of the day should consist of chopped beef (preferably raw). The amount needed will vary from about three tablespoonfuls for Toy breeds up to one-half cupful for large breeds. The other meal should consist of equal parts of chopped beef and strained, cooked vegetables to which is added a little dry toast. (If you plan eventually to feed your dog canned food or dog meal, it can gradually be introduced at this meal.) Cod-liver oil and dicalcium phosphate should be mixed with the food for this meal. The amount of each will vary from one-half teaspoonful for Toys to 1 tablespoonful for large breeds.

The amount of food offered at each meal must gradually be increased and by five months the puppy will require about twice what he needed at three months. Puppies should be fat, and it is best to let them eat as much as they want at each meal, so long as they are hungry again when it is time for the next feeding. Any food not eaten within fifteen minutes should be taken away. With a little attention to the dog's eating habits, the owner can prepare enough food and still not waste any.

When the puppy is five months old, the final feeding of the day can be eliminated and the five meals compressed into four so the puppy still receives the same quantities and types of food. At six or seven months, the four meals can be compressed into three. By the time a puppy of small or medium breed is eleven to twelve months old, feedings can be reduced to two meals a day. At the end of the first year, cod-liver oil and dicalcium phosphate can usually be discontinued.

Large breeds mature more slowly and three meals a day are usually necessary until eighteen or twenty-four months of age. Cod-liver oil and dicalcium phosphate should be continued, too, until the large dog reaches maturity.

A mature dog usually eats slightly less than he did as a growing puppy. For mature dogs, one large meal a day is usually sufficient, although some owners prefer to give two meals. As long as the dog enjoys optimum health and is neither too fat nor too thin, the number of meals a day makes little difference.

The amount of food required for mature dogs will vary. With canned dog food or home-prepared foods (that is, the combination of meat, vegetables, and meal), the approximate amount required is one-half ounce of food per pound of body weight. Thus, about eight ounces of such foods would be needed each day for a mature dog weighing sixteen pounds. If the dog is fed a dehydrated commercial food, approximately one ounce of food is needed for each pound of body weight. Approximately one pound of dry food per day would be required by a dog weighing sixteen pounds. Most manufacturers of commercial foods provide information on packages as to approximate daily needs of various breeds.

As a dog becomes older and less active, he may become too fat. Or his appetite may decrease so he becomes too thin. It is necessary to adjust the diet in either case, for the dog will live longer and enjoy better health if he is maintained in trim condition. The simplest way to decrease or increase body weight is by decreasing or increasing the amount of fat in the diet. Protein content should be maintained at a high level throughout the dog's life, although the amount of food at each meal can be decreased if the dog becomes too fat.

If the older dog becomes reluctant to eat, it may be necessary to coax him with special food he normally relishes. Warming the food will increase its aroma and usually will help to entice the dog to eat. If he still refuses, rubbing some of the food on the dog's lips and gums may stimulate interest. It may be helpful also to offer food in smaller amounts and increase the number of meals per day. Foods that are highly nutritious and easily digested are especially desirable for older dogs. Small amounts of cooked, ground liver, cottage cheese, or mashed, hard-cooked eggs should be included in the diet often.

Before a bitch is bred, her owner should make sure that she is in optimum condition—slightly on the lean side rather than fat. The bitch in whelp is given much the same diet she was fed prior to breeding, with slight increases in amounts of meat, liver, and dairy products. Beginning about six weeks after breeding, she should be fed two meals per day rather than one, and the total daily intake increased. (Some bitches in whelp require as much as 50% more food than they consume normally.) She must not be permitted to become fat, for whelping problems are more likely to occur in overweight dogs. Cod-liver oil and dicalcium phosphate should be provided until after the puppies are weaned. The amount of each will vary from one-half teaspoonful to one tablespoonful a day, depending upon her size.

The dog used only occasionally for breeding will not require a special diet, but he should be well fed and maintained in optimum condition. A dog that is at public stud and used frequently may require a slightly increased amount of food. But his basic diet will require no change so long as his general health is good and his flesh is firm and hard.

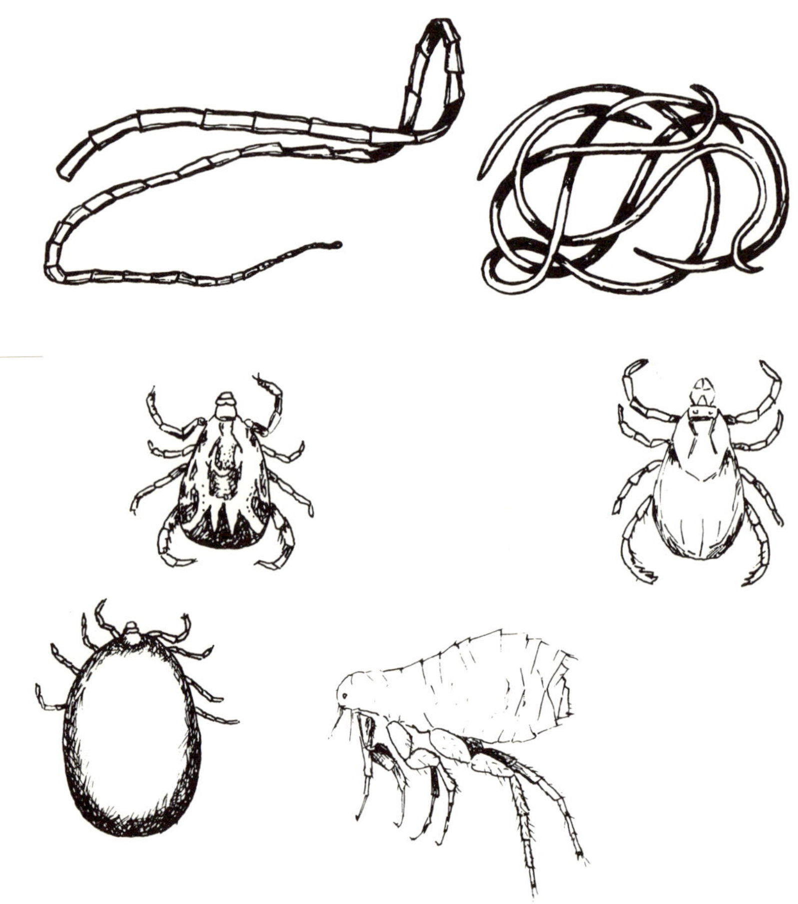

Some common internal and external parasites.

(UPPER LEFT) Tape worm. (UPPER RIGHT) Round worms. (CENTER) American dog ticks—left, female and right, male (much enlarged). (LOWER LEFT) Female tick engorged. (LOWER RIGHT) dog flea (much enlarged).

Maintaining the Dog's Health

Proper nutrition is essential in maintaining the dog's resistance to infectious diseases, in reducing susceptibility to organic diseases, and, of course, in preventing dietary deficiency diseases.

Rickets is probably the most common deficiency disease and afflicts puppies not provided sufficient calcium and Vitamin D. Bones fail to calcify properly, development of teeth is retarded, joints become knobby and deformed, and muscles are flabby. Symptoms include lameness, arching of neck and back, and a tendency of the legs to bow. Treatment consists of providing adequate amounts of dicalcium phosphate and Vitamin D and exposing the dog to sunlight. If detected and treated before reaching an advanced stage, bone damage may be lessened somewhat, although it cannot be corrected completely.

Osteomalacia, similar to rickets, may occur in adult dogs. Treatment is the same as for rickets, but here, too, prevention is preferable to cure. Permanent deformities resulting from rickets or osteomalacia will not be inherited, so once victims recover, they can be used for breeding.

To prevent the growth of disease-producing bacteria and other micro-organisms, cleanliness is essential. All equipment, especially water and food dishes, must be kept immaculately clean. Cleanliness is also essential in controlling external parasites, which thrive in unsanitary surroundings.

Fleas, lice, mites, and ticks can be eradicated in the dog's quarters by regular use of one of the insecticide sprays with a four to six weeks' residual effect. Bedding, blankets, and pillows should be laundered frequently and treated with an insecticide containing rotenone or DDT. Treatment for external parasites varies, depending upon the parasite involved, but a number of good dips and powders are available at pet stores.

Fleas may be eliminated by using a flea powder containing lindane. The coat must be dusted thoroughly with the powder at frequent intervals during the summer months when fleas are a problem. For eradicating lice, dips containing rotenone or DDT must be applied to the coat. A fine-toothed comb should then be used to remove dead lice and eggs, which are firmly attached to the coat. Mites live deep in the ear canal, producing irritation to the lining of the ear and causing a brownish-black, dry type discharge. Plain mineral oil or ear ointment should be swabbed on the inner surface of the ear twice a week until mites are eliminated. Ticks may carry Rocky Mountain spotted fever, so, to avoid possible infection, they should be removed from the dog only with tweezers and should be destroyed by burning (or by dropping them into insecticide). Heavy infestation can be controlled by sponging the coat daily with a solution containing a special tick dip.

Among preparations available for controlling parasites on the dog's body are some that can be given internally. Since dosage must be carefully controlled, these preparations should not be used without consulting a veterinarian.

Internal parasites, with the exception of the tapeworm, may be transmitted from a mother dog to the puppies. Infestation may also result from contact with infected bedding or through access to a yard where an infected dog relieves himself. The types that may infest dogs are roundworms, whipworms, tapeworms, hookworms, and heartworms. All cause similar symptoms: a generally unthrifty appearance, stary coat, dull eyes, weakness and emaciation despite a ravenous appetite, coughing, vomiting, diarrhea, and sometimes bloody stools. Not all symptoms are present in every case, of course.

Promiscuous dosing for worms is dangerous and different types of worms require different treatment. So if you suspect your dog has worms, ask your veterinarian to make a microscopic examination of the feces, and to prescribe appropriate treatment if evidence of worm infestation is found.

Clogged anal glands cause intense discomfort, which the dog may attempt to relieve by scooting himself along the floor on his haunches. These glands, located on either side of the anus, secrete a substance that enables the dog to expel the contents of the rectum. If they become clogged, they may give the dog an unpleasant odor and when neglected, serious infection may result. Contents of the glands can be easily expelled into a wad of

cotton, which should be held under the tail with the left hand.
Then, using the right hand, pressure should be exerted with the
thumb on one side of the anus, the forefinger on the other. The
normal secretion is brownish in color, with an unpleasant odor.
The presence of blood or pus indicates infection and should be
called to the attention of a veterinarian.

Fits, often considered a symptom of worms, may result from
a variety of causes, including vitamin deficiencies, or playing to
the point of exhaustion. A veterinarian should be consulted when
a fit occurs, for it may be a symptom of serious illness.

Distemper takes many and varied forms, so it is sometimes
difficult for even experienced veterinarians to diagnose. It is the
number one killer of dogs, and although it is not unknown in
older dogs, its victims are usually puppies. While some dogs do
recover, permanent damage to the brain or nervous system is
often sustained. Symptoms may include lethargy, diarrhea, vomiting, reduced appetite, cough, nasal discharge, inflammation of
the eyes, and a rise in temperature. If distemper is suspected, a
veterinarian must be consulted at once, for early treatment is
essential. Effective preventive measures lie in inoculation. Shots
for temporary immunity should be given all puppies within a few
weeks after whelping, and the permanent inoculations should be
given as soon thereafter as possible.

Hardpad has been fairly prevalent in Great Britain for a number of years, and its incidence in the United States is increasing. Symptoms are similar to those of distemper, but as the disease progresses, the pads of the feet harden and eventually peel. Chances of recovery are not favorable unless prompt veterinary care is secured.

Infectious hepatitis in dogs affects the liver, as does the human form, but apparently is not transmissible to man. Symptoms are similar to those of distemper, and the disease rapidly reaches the acute stage. Since hepatitis is often fatal, prompt veterinary treatment is essential. Effective vaccines are available and should be provided all puppies. A combination distemper-hepatitis vaccine is sometimes used.

Leptospirosis is caused by a micro-organism often transmitted by contact with rats, or by ingestion of food contaminated by rats. The disease can be transmitted to man, so anyone caring for an afflicted dog must take steps to avoid infection. Symptoms include vomiting, loss of appetite, diarrhea, fever, depression and lethargy, redness of eyes and gums, and sometimes jaundice. Since permanent kidney damage may result, veterinary treatment should be secured immediately.

Rabies is a disease that is always fatal—and it is transmissible to man. It is caused by a virus that attacks the nervous system and is present in the saliva of an infected animal. When an infected animal bites another, the virus is transmitted to the new victim. It may also enter the body through cuts and scratches that come in contact with saliva containing the virus.

All warm-blooded animals are subject to rabies and it may be transmitted by foxes, skunks, squirrels, horses, and cattle as well as dogs. Anyone bitten by a dog (or other animal) should see his physician immediately, and health and law enforcement officials should be notified. Also, if your dog is bitten by another animal, consult your veterinarian immediately.

In most areas, rabies shots are required by law. Even if not required, all dogs should be given anti-rabies vaccine, for it is an effective preventive measure.

Injuries of a serious nature—deep cuts, broken bones, severe burns, etc.—always require veterinary care. However, the dog may need first aid before being moved to a veterinary hospital.

A dog injured in any way should be approached cautiously, for reactions of a dog in pain are unpredictable and he may bite even a beloved master. A muzzle should always be applied before any attempt is made to move the dog or treat him in any way. The muzzle can be improvised from a strip of cloth, bandage, or even heavy cord, looped firmly around the dog's jaws and tied under the lower jaw. The ends should then be extended back of the neck and tied again so the loop around the jaws will stay in place.

A stretcher for moving a heavy dog can be improvised from a rug or board—preferably two people should be available to transport it. A small dog can be carried by one person simply by grasping the loose skin at the nape of the neck with one hand and placing the other hand under the dog's hips.

Severe bleeding from a leg can be controlled by applying a tourniquet between the wound and the body, but the tourniquet must be loosened at ten-minute intervals. Severe bleeding from head or body can be controlled by placing a cloth or gauze pad over the wound, then applying firm pressure with the hand.

To treat minor cuts, first trim the hair from around the wound, then wash the area with warm soapy water and apply a mild antiseptic such as tincture of metaphen.

Shock is usually the aftermath of severe injury and requires immediate veterinary attention. The dog appears dazed, lips and tongue are pale, and breathing is shallow. The dog should be wrapped in blankets and kept warm, and if possible, kept lying down with his head lower than his body.

Fractures require immediate professional attention. A broken bone should be immobilized while the dog is transported to the veterinarian but no attempt should be made to splint it.

Burns from hot liquid or hot metals should be treated by applying a bland ointment, provided the burned area is small. Burns over large areas should be treated by a veterinarian.

Burns from chemicals should first be treated by flushing the coat with plain water, taking care to protect the dog's eyes and ears. A baking soda solution can then be applied to neutralize the chemical further. If the burned area is small, a bland ointment should be applied. If the burned area is large, more extensive treatment will be required, as well as veterinary care.

Poisoning is more often accidental than deliberate, but whichever the case, symptoms and treatment are the same. If the poisoning is not discovered immediately, the dog may be found unconscious. His mouth will be slimy, he will tremble, have difficulty breathing, and possibly go into convulsions. Veterinary treatment must be secured immediately.

If you find the dog cating something you know to be poisonous, induce vomiting immediately by repeatedly forcing the dog to swallow a mixture of equal parts of hydrogen peroxide and water. Delay of even a few minutes may result in death. When the contents of the stomach have been emptied, force the dog to swallow raw egg white, which will slow absorption of the poison. Then call the veterinarian. Provide him with information as to the type of poison, and follow his advice as to further treatment.

Some chemicals are toxic even though not swallowed, so before using a product, make sure it can be used safely around pets.

Electric shock usually results because an owner negligently leaves an electric cord exposed where the dog can chew on it. If possible, disconnect the cord before touching the dog. Otherwise, yank the cord from the dog's mouth so you will not receive a shock when you try to help him. If the dog is unconscious, artificial respiration and stimulants will be required, so a veterinarian should be consulted at once.

Eye problems of a minor nature—redness or occasional discharge—may be treated with a few drops of boric acid solution (2%) or salt solution (1 teaspoonful table salt to 1 pint sterile water). Cuts on the eyeball, bruises close to the eyes, or persistent discharge shoud be treated only by a veterinarian.

Skin problems usually cause persistent itching. However, *follicular mange* does not usually do so but is evidenced by moth-eaten-looking patches, especially about the head and along the back. *Sarcoptic mange* produces severe itching and is evidenced by patchy, crusty areas on body, legs, and abdomen. Any evidence suggesting either should be called to the attention of a veterinarian. Both require extensive treatment and both may be contracted by humans.

Eczema is characterized by extreme itching, redness of the skin and exudation of serous matter. It may result from a variety of causes, and the exact cause in a particular case may be difficult to determine. Relief may be secured by dusting the dog twice a week with a soothing powder containing a fungicide and an insecticide.

Allergies are not readily distinguished from other skin troubles except through laboratory tests. However, dog owners should be alert to the fact that straw, shavings, or newspapers used for bedding, various coat dressings and shampoos, or simply bathing the dog too often, may produce allergic skin reactions in some dogs. Thus, a change in dog-keeping practices often relieves them.

Symptoms of illness may be so obvious there is no question that the dog is ill, or so subtle that the owner isn't sure whether there is a change from normal or not. *Loss of appetite, malaise* (general lack of interest in what is going on), *and vomiting* may be ignored if they occur singly and persist only for a day. However, in combination with other evidence of illness, such symptoms may be significant and the dog should be watched closely. *Abnormal bowel movements,* especially diarrhea or bloody stools, are cause for immediate concern. *Urinary abnormalities* may indicate infections, and bloody urine is always an indication of a serious condition. When a dog that has long been housebroken suddenly becomes incontinent, a veterinarian should be consulted, for he may be able to suggest treatment or medication that will be helpful.

Persistent coughing is often considered a symptom of worms, but may also indicate heart trouble—especially in older dogs.

Vomiting is another symptom often attributed to worm infestation. Dogs suffering from indigestion sometimes eat grass, apparently to induce vomiting and relieve discomfort.

Stary coat—dull and lackluster—indicates generally poor health and possible worm infestation. *Dull eyes* may result from similar conditions. Certain forms of blindness may also cause the eyes to lose the sparkle of vibrant good health.

Fever is a positive indication of illness and consistent deviation from the normal temperature range of 100 to 102 degrees is cause for concern. To take the dog's temperature, first place the dog on his side. Coat the bulb of a rectal thermometer with petroleum jelly, raise the dog's tail, insert the thermometer to approximately half its length, and hold it in position for two minutes. Clean the thermometer with rubbing alcohol after each use and be sure to shake it down.

A dog that is seriously ill, requiring surgical treatment, transfusions, or intravenous feeding, must be hospitalized. One requiring less complicated treatment is better cared for at home, but it is essential that the dog be kept in a quiet environment. Preferably, his bed should be in a room apart from family activity, yet close at hand, so his condition can be checked frequently. Clean bedding and adequate warmth are essential, as are a constant supply of fresh, cool water, and foods to tempt the appetite.

Special equipment is not ordinarily needed, but the following items will be useful in caring for a sick dog, as well as in giving first aid for injuries:

petroleum jelly	tincture of metaphen
rubbing alcohol	cotton, gauze, and adhesive tape
mineral oil	burn ointment
rectal thermometer	tweezers
hydrogen peroxide	boric acid solution (2%)

If special medication is prescribed, it may be administered in any one of several ways. A pill or small capsule may be concealed in a small piece of meat, which the dog will usually swallow with no problem. A large capsule may be given by holding the dog's mouth open, inserting the capsule as far as possible down the throat, then holding the mouth closed until the dog swallows. Liquid medicine should be measured into a small bottle or test tube. Then, if the corner of the dog's lip is pulled out while the head is tilted upward, the liquid can be poured between the lips and teeth, a small amount at a time. If he refuses to swallow, keeping the dog's head tilted and stroking his throat will usually induce swallowing.

Foods offered the sick dog should be particularly nutritious and easily digested. Meals should be smaller than usual and offered at more frequent intervals. If the dog is reluctant to eat, offer food he particularly likes and warm it slightly to increase aroma and thus make it more tempting.

Housing Your Dog

Every dog should have a bed of his own, snug and warm, where he can retire undisturbed when he wishes to nap. And, especially with a small puppy, it is desirable to have the bed arranged so the dog can be securely confined at times, safe and contented. If the puppy is taught early in life to stay quietly in his box at night, or when the family is out, the habit will carry over into adulthood and will benefit both dog and master.

The dog should never be banished to a damp, cold basement, but should be quartered in an out-of-the-way corner close to the center of family activity. His bed can be an elaborate cushioned affair with electric warming pad, or simply a rectangular wooden box or heavy paper carton, cushioned with a clean cotton rug or towel. Actually, the latter is ideal for a new puppy, for it is snug, easy to clean, and expendable. A "door" can be cut on one side of the box for easy access, but it should be placed in such a way that the dog can still be confined when desirable.

The shipping crates used by professional handlers at dog shows make ideal indoor quarters. They are lightweight but strong, provide adequate air circulation, yet are snug and warm and easily cleaned. For the dog owner who takes his dog along when he travels, a dog crate is ideal, for the dog will willingly stay in his accustomed bed during long automobile trips, and the crate can be taken inside motels or hotels at night, making the dog a far more acceptable guest.

Dog crates are made of chromed metal or wood, and some have tops covered with a special rubber matting so they can be used as grooming tables. Anyone moderately handy with tools can construct a crate similar to the one illustrated on page 35.

Crates come in various sizes, to suit various breeds of dogs. For reasons of economy, the size selected for a puppy should be adequate for use when the dog is full grown. If the area seems too large when the puppy is small, a temporary cardboard partition can be installed to limit the area he occupies.

The dog owner who lives in the suburbs or in the country may want to keep a mature dog outdoors part of the time, in which case an outdoor doghouse should be provided. This type of kennel can also be constructed by the home handyman, but must be more substantial than quarters used indoors.

Outside finish of the doghouse can be of any type, but double wall construction will make for greater warmth in chilly weather. The floor should be smooth and easy to clean, so tongued and grooved boards or plywood are best. To keep the floor from contact with the damp earth, supports should be laid flat on the ground, running lengthwise of the structure. 2 x 4s serve well as supports for doghouses for small or medium breeds, but 4 x 4s should be used for large breeds.

The outdoor kennel must be big enough so that the dog can turn around inside, but small enough so that his body heat will keep it warm in chilly weather. The overall length of the kennel shoud be twice the length of the adult dog, measured from tip of nose to onset of tail. Width of the structure should be approximately three-fourths the length. And height from the floor to the point where the roof begins should be approximately one and a half the adult dog's height at the shoulders. If you build the house when the dog is still a puppy, you can determine his approximate adult size by referring to the Standard for his breed.

An "A" type roof is preferable, and an overhang of six inches all the way around will provide protection from sun and rain. If the roof is hinged to fold back, the interior of the kennel can be cleaned readily.

The entrance should be placed to one side rather than in the center, which will provide further protection against the weather. One of the commercially made door closures of rubber will keep out rain, snow, and wind, yet give the pet complete freedom to enter and leave his home.

The best location for the doghouse is where it will get enough morning sun to keep it dry, yet will not be in full sun during hot afternoons. If possible, the back of the doghouse should be placed toward the prevailing winds.

A fenced run or yard is essential to the outdoor kennel, and the fence must be sturdy enough that the dog cannot break through it, and high enough so he cannot jump or climb over it. The gate should have a latch of a type that can't be opened accidentally. The area enclosed must provide the dog with space to exercise freely, or else the dog must be exercised on the leash every day, for no dog should be confined to a tiny yard day after day without adequate exercise.

The yard must be kept clean and odor free, and the doghouse must be scrubbed and disinfected at frequent intervals. One of the insecticides made especially for use in kennels—one with a four to six weeks' residual effect—should be used regularly on floors and walls, inside and out.

Enough bedding must be provided so the dog can snuggle into it and keep warm in chilly weather. Bedding should either be of a type that is inexpensive, so it can be discarded and replaced frequently, or of a type that can be laundered readily. Dogs are often allergic to fungi found on straw, hay, or grass, and sometimes newspaper ink, but cedar shavings and old cotton rugs and blankets usually serve very well.

The Stone-age Dog

A Spotted Dog from India, "Parent of the Modern Coach dog."

History of
the Genus Canis

The history of man's association with the dog is a fascinating one, extending into the past at least seventy centuries, and involving the entire history of civilized man from the early Stone Age to the present.

The dog, technically a member of the genus *Canis,* belongs to the zoological family group *Canidae,* which also includes such animals as wolves, foxes, jackals, and coyotes. In the past it was generally agreed that the dog resulted from the crossing of various members of the family *Canidae.* Recent findings have amended this theory somewhat, and most authorities now feel the jackal probably has no direct relationship with the dog. Some believe dogs are descended from wolves and foxes, with the wolf the main progenitor. As evidence, they cite the fact that the teeth of the wolf are identical in every detail with those of the dog, whereas the teeth of the jackal are totally different.

Still other authorities insist that the dog always has existed as a separate and distinct animal. This group admits that it is possible for a dog to mate with a fox, coyote, or wolf, but points out that the resulting puppies are unable to breed with each other, although they can breed with stock of the same genus as either parent. Therefore, they insist, it was impossible for a new and distinct genus to have developed from such crossings. They then cite the fact that any dog can be mated with any other dog and the progeny bred among themselves. These researchers point out, too, heritable characteristics that are totally different in the three animals. For instance, the pupil of the dog's eye is round, that of the wolf oblique, and that of the jackal vertical. Tails, too, differ considerably, for tails of foxes, coyotes, and wolves always drop behind them, while those of dogs may be carried over the back or straight up.

Much conjecture centers on two wild dog species that still exist—the Dingo of Australia, and the Dhole in India. Similar in appearance, both are reddish in color, both have rather long, slender jaws, both have rounded ears that stand straight up, and both species hunt in packs. Evidence indicates that they had the same ancestors. Yet, today, they live in areas that are more than 4,000 miles apart.

Despite the fact that it is impossible to determine just when the dog first appeared as a distinct species, archeologists have found definite proof that the dog was the first animal domesticated by man. When man lived by tracking, trapping, and killing game, the dog added to the forces through which man discovered and captured the quarry. Man shared his primitive living quarters with the dog, and the two together devoured the prey. Thus, each helped to sustain the life of the other. The dog assisted man, too, by defending the campsite against marauders. As man gradually became civilized, the dog's usefulness was extended to guarding the other animals man domesticated, and, even before the wheel was invented, the dog served as a beast of burden. In fact, archeological findings show that aboriginal peoples of Switzerland and Ireland used the dog for such purposes long before they learned to till the soil.

Cave drawings from the palaeolithic era, which was the earliest part of the Old World Stone Age, include hunting scenes in which a rough, canine-like form is shown alongside huntsmen. One of these drawings is believed to be 50,000 years old, and gives credence to the theory that all dogs are descended from a primitive type ancestor that was neither fox nor wolf.

Archeological findings show that Europeans of the New Stone Age possessed a breed of dogs of wolf-like appearance, and a similar breed has been traced through the successive Bronze Age and Iron Age. Accurate details are not available, though, as to the external appearance of domesticated dogs prior to historic times (roughly four to five thousand years ago).

Early records in Chaldean and Egyptian tombs show that several distinct and well-established dog types had been developed by about 3700 B.C. Similar records show that the early people of the Nile Valley regarded the dog as a god, often burying it as a mummy in special cemeteries and mourning its death.

Some of the early Egyptian dogs had been given names, such as Akna, Tarn, and Abu, and slender dogs of the Greyhound type and a short-legged Terrier type are depicted in drawings found

Bas-relief of Hunters with Nets and Mastiffs. From the walls of Assurbanipal's palace at Nineveh 668-626 B.C. *British Museum.*

in Egyptian royal tombs that are at least 5,000 years old. The Afghan Hound and the Saluki are shown in drawings of only slightly later times. Another type of ancient Egyptian dog was much heavier and more powerful, with short coat and massive head. These probably hunted by scent, as did still another type of Egyptian dog that had a thick furry coat, a tail curled almost flat over the back, and erect "prick" ears.

Early Romans and Greeks mentioned their dogs often in literature, and both made distinctions between those that hunted by sight and those that hunted by scent. The Romans' canine classifications were similar to those we use now. In addition to dogs comparable to the Greek sight and scent hounds, the ancient Romans had Canes *villatici* (housedogs) and Canes *pastorales* (sheepdogs), corresponding to our present-day working dogs.

The dog is mentioned many times in the Old Testament. The first reference, in Genesis, leads some Biblical scholars to assert that man and dog have been companions from the time man was created. And later Biblical references bring an awareness of the diversity in breeds and types existing thousands of years ago.

As civilization advanced, man found new uses for dogs. Some required great size and strength. Others needed less of these characteristics but greater agility and better sight. Still others needed an accentuated sense of smell. As time went on, men kept those puppies that suited specific purposes especially well and bred them together. Through ensuing generations of selective breeding, desirable characteristics appeared with increasing frequency. Dogs used in a particular region for a special purpose gradually became more like each other, yet less like dogs of other areas used for different purposes. Thus were established the foundations for the various breeds we have today.

The American Kennel Club, the leading dog organization in the United States, divides the various breeds into six "Groups," based on similarity of purposes for which they were developed.

"Sporting Dogs" include the Pointers, Setters, Spaniels, and Retrievers that were developed by sportsmen interested in hunting game birds. Most of the Pointers and Setters are of comparatively recent origin. Their development parallels the development of sporting firearms, and most of them evolved in the British Isles. Exceptions are the Weimaraner, which was developed in Germany, and the Vizsla, or Hungarian Pointer, believed to have been developed by the Magyar hordes that swarmed over Central Europe a thousand years ago. The Irish were among the first to use Spaniels, though the name indicates that the original stock may have come from Spain. Two Sporting breeds, the American Water Spaniel, and the Chesapeake Bay Retriever, were developed entirely in the United States.

"Hounds," among which are Dachshunds, Beagles, Bassets, Harriers, and Foxhounds, are used singly, in pairs, or in packs to "course" (or run) and hunt for rabbits, foxes, and various rodents. But little larger, the Norwegian Elkhound is used in its native country to hunt big game—moose, bear, and deer.

The smaller Hound breeds hunt by scent, while the Irish Wolfhound, Borzoi, Scottish Deerhound, Saluki, and Greyhound hunt by sight. The Whippet, Saluki, and Greyhound are notably fleet of foot, and racing these breeds (particularly the Greyhound) is popular sport.

The Bloodhound is a member of the Hound Group that is known world-wide for its scenting ability. On the other hand, the Basenji is a comparatively rare Hound breed and has the distinction of being the only dog that cannot bark.

"Working Dogs" have the greatest utilitarian value of all modern dogs and contribute to man's welfare in diverse ways. The Boxer, Doberman Pinscher, Rottweiler, German Shepherd, Great Dane, and Giant Schnauzer are often trained to serve as sentries and aid police in patrolling streets. The German Shepherd is especially noted as a guide dog for the blind. The Collie, the various breeds of Sheepdogs, and the two Corgi breeds are known throughout the world for their extraordinary herding ability. And the exploits of the St. Bernard and Newfoundland are legendary, their records for saving lives unsurpassed.

The Siberian Husky and the Alaskan Malamute are noted for tremendous strength and stamina. Had it not been for these hardy Northern breeds, the great polar expeditions might never have taken place, for Admiral Byrd used these dogs to reach points inaccessible by other means. Even today, with our jet-age transportation, the Northern breeds provide a more practical means of travel in frigid areas than do modern machines.

"Terriers" derive their name from the Latin *terra,* meaning

1. The Newfoundland. 2. The English Setter. 3. The Large Water-spaniel. 4. The Terrier. 5. The Cur-dog. 6. The Shepherd's Dog. 7. The Bulldog. 8. The Mastiff. 9. The Greenland Dog. 10. The Rought Water-dog. 11. The Small Water-spaniel. 12. The Old English Hound. 13. The Dalmatian or Coach-dog. 14. The Comporter (very much of a Papillon). 15. "Toy Dog, Bottle, Glass, and Pipe." *From a vignette.* 16. The Springer or Cocker. *From Thomas Bewick's "General History of Quadrupeds" (1790).*

"earth," for all of the breeds in this Group are fond of burrowing. Terriers hunt by digging into the earth to rout rodents and fur-bearing animals such as badgers, woodchucks, and otters. Some breeds are expected merely to force the animals from their dens in order that the hunter can complete the capture. Others are expected to find and destroy the prey, either on the surface or under the ground.

Terriers come in a wide variety of sizes, ranging from such large breeds as the Airedale and Kerry Blue to such small ones as the Skye, the Dandie Dinmont, the West Highland White, and the Scottish Terrier. England, Ireland, and Scotland produced most of the Terrier breeds, although the Miniature Schnauzer was developed in Germany.

"Toys," as the term indicates, are small breeds. Although they make little claim to usefulness other than as ideal housepets, Toy dogs develop as much protective instinct as do larger breeds and serve effectively in warning of the approach of strangers.

Origins of the Toys are varied. The Pekingese was developed as the royal dog of China more than two thousand years before the birth of Christ. The Chihuahua, smallest of the Toys, originated in Mexico and is believed to be a descendant of the Techichi, a dog of great religious significance to the Aztecs, while the Italian Greyhound was popular in the days of ancient Pompeii.

"Non-Sporting Dogs" include a number of popular breeds of varying ancestry. The Standard and Miniature Poodles were developed in France for the purpose of retrieving game from water. The Bulldog originated in Great Britain and was bred for the purpose of "baiting" bulls. The Chowchow apparently originated centuries ago in China, for it is pictured in a bas relief dated to the Han dynasty of about 150 B.C.

The Dalmatian served as a carriage dog in Dalmatia, protecting travelers in bandit-infested regions. The Keeshond, recognized as the national dog of Holland, is believed to have originated in the Arctic or possibly the Sub-Arctic. The Schipperke, sometimes erroneously described as a Dutch dog, originated in the Flemish provinces of Belgium. And the Lhasa Apso came from Tibet, where it is known as "Abso Seng Kye," the "Bark Lion Sentinel Dog."

During the thousands of years that man and dog have been closely associated, a strong affinity has been built up between the two. The dog has more than earned his way as a helper, and his faithful, selfless devotion to man is legendary. The ways in which the dog has proved his intelligence, his courage, and his dependability in situations of stress are amply recorded in the countless tales of canine heroism that highlight the pages of history, both past and present.

Dogs in Woodcuts. (*1st row*) (LEFT) "Maltese dog with shorter hair"; (RIGHT) "Spotted sporting dog trained to catch game"; (*2nd row*) (LEFT) Sporting white dog; (RIGHT) "Spanish dog with floppy ears": (*3rd row*) (LEFT) "French dog"; (RIGHT) "Mad dog of Grevinus"; (*4th row*) (LEFT) Hairy Maltese dog; (RIGHT) "English fighting dog . . . of horrid aspect." *From Aldrovandus (1637).*

History of the Lhasa Apso

There are a number of breeds originating in the Orient that have similar characteristics. While there is a degree of similarity, there is also a good deal of difference in size and in quantity of coat. It is possible to hypothesize that all these breeds came from common ancestors and that the differences that exist today are the result of breedings that took place with no thought to maintaining consistency of type.

Oriental breeds have the foreshortened face and the tail carried high over the back, usually curled. In addition to the Lhasa Apso, there are the Shih Tzu, the Pekingese, the Tibetan Spaniel, the Japanese Spaniel, the Tibetan Terrier, the Tibetan Mastiff, and the Chow Chow.

There seems to be a close relationship in conformation between the Lhasa Apso and the Shih Tzu, the Tibetan Spaniel, the Japanese Spaniel, and the Tibetan Terrier. The Lhasa Apso and the Shih Tzu are quite similar and were undoubtedly even more so a century or two ago. The Pekingese is similar in certain respects, differing mainly in coat and gait. The Tibetan Spaniel and the Japanese Spaniel differ from the Lhasa Apso in head and coat. The Tibetan Terrier has certain characteristics similar to those of the Tibetan Spaniel but is larger and has a Terrier-type head.

The Chow Chow, while coming from the Orient, is really in a different category from the Lhasa Apso. Size puts the Chow Chow in a different class, although the foreshortened muzzle and the tail do appear to link the Chow Chow and the smaller Orientals.

The breed that today is known in the United States as the Lhasa Apso dates back a thousand years or more in Tibet, the country of its origin. While recorded history of the Lhasa Apso is most difficult to verify, there are strong indications that the breed is among the oldest in the world.

Because of the almost complete isolation of Tibet, little was known about it by the outside world. The Lhasa Apso, moreover, belonged only to the Dalai Lama or to the rulers of other monasteries. They were kept hidden and well protected from strangers

A wood carving of a Lhasa Apso, by the Mexican sculptor José Pinal.

and were seen only by those who had the privilege of entering the monasteries and the sacred villages. Early travelers, not enjoying this special privilege, were, therefore, completely unaware of the existence of the sacred little dogs.

The word *Apso,* which has almost always been associated with the breed, is a corruption of the Tibetan word *rapso,* which is an adjective meaning shaggy or goat-like. The Lhasa Apso certainly is a shaggy little dog and his goat-like characteristics can be seen when he is at play, leaping from one object to another. His surefootedness and his ability to leap justify the use of the word *rapso.*

Being the inside watch dog of the Potala Palace of the Dalai Lama, the Lhasa Apso was trained as a warning guard for the pro-

A needle point piano bench cover showing Ch. Maytime Princess O'Berano, Yorkshire Terrier Ch. Yorkfold on Target, and Ch. Orlane's Tiger Burning Bright.

tection of his master. He was taught to distinguish between the residents of the monastery and strangers. He learned very quickly to greet all visitors with nervous and hostile barking. His innate intelligence and keen sense of hearing made him a "natural" as a sentry dog trained to detect the familiar from the unfamiliar and to give warning when he felt it necessary.

While certain qualities of conformation such as color were regarded as important, the Lhasa was really considered an obedience type of dog since his role and training were intended to serve a special function in the palace. This lack of special interest in conformation resulted in a great variety of sizes. The lack of uniformity in the breeding program genetically locked certain variables into the breed, which helps to explain the "throwbacks" that appear even today in carefully controlled breeding programs of professional Lhasa Apso breeders.

Great uniformity in the conformation aspect of breeding has, however, been achieved today in the United States. So much care has gone into genetic studies made by certain breeders that their kennel line is immediately identifiable in the show ring. This is great testimony to their professionalism. That qualities of conformation are of prime importance today is evidenced by the fact that very few Lhasa Apsos are seen in the obedience rings. This does not indicate a lack of the qualities necessary for obedience work, but rather a greater interest in other aspects of showing.

Among the characteristics the Lhasa Apso shares with other breeds of Tibetan origin are the dense coat and the curly tail carried up and over the back. Dogs living in a cold climate and at a high altitude developed dense coats through the process of natural evolution. Three other Tibetan breeds of dogs share the same coat and tail characteristics—the Tibetan Terrier, the Tibetan Spaniel, and the Tibetan Mastiff.

The Tibetan Mastiff, because of its size, served as the outside guard dog for the lamaseries and the homes of the wealthy. The Tibetan Spaniel was considered primarily a beautiful lap dog, admired for its looks rather than for any function it might serve. The Tibetan Terrier was the most common breed, for it was raised in many parts of Tibet. It is the true Terrier representative, both in disposition and conformation.

The Lhasa Apso was known in its native land as Abso Seng Kye or the Bark Sentinel Lion Dog or simply the Lion Dog. When it was brought to England it was first called the Talisman Dog, the Shen Tron, or the Lhasa Terrier. It was for some time even referred to as the Tibetan Apso.

From the sixteenth to the twentieth centuries, when Tibet owed both its safety and its existence to the good relations with the government of China, the Lhasa Apso was used to pay special tribute to members of the Chinese royal family—the Manchu Dynasty. Pairs of Lhasa Apsos were sent to members of the royal family and other influential dignitaries as tribute. According to tradition, the Lhasa Apso brought good luck and happiness to its new owner —and what better way could a subject show deference to an emperor.

With the fall of the Manchu Dynasty, the Lhasa Apso, in isolated instances, made an occasional appearance in the Western world. It first appeared in England at the very beginning of this century, having been brought back by a Colonel R. C. Duncan, who had been stationed in the Far East during a tour of military duty. Little interest was generated by those first dogs or by the very limited number that arrived during the next three or four decades.

It was not until just before World War II that Lhasa Apsos were seen in sufficient numbers to be recognized readily. The war, however, prevented any great growth in popularity for obvious reasons.

Credit for the prestige the Lhasa Apso now enjoys in the United States belongs primarily to one man who did more than any other in establishing a breeding line and in bringing recognition to the breed. C. Suydam Cutting, a gentleman of means and a world traveler, spent the years following World War I roaming the world with the famous men of his generation. In 1925 one such expedition to the Far East was made with the brother of former President Theodore Roosevelt. During this particular trip, Mr. Cutting received only a superficial introduction to Tibet, but it served to whet his appetite. On a subsequent trip he had an audience with the Thirteenth Dalai Lama, with whom he was able to maintain a friendship that spanned a period of years.

Their friendship resulted in an exchange of gifts, and in 1933 the

An oil painting of a Tibetan boy and his Lhasa Apso. This painting is from the collection of Miss Grace Walther and Dr. Esther Fritz, who served as medical missionaries to Tibet for twenty-five years.

Dalai Lama sent a pair of Lhasa Apsos to the Cuttings. The male was called Taikoo and was a parti-colored black and white. The female, Dinkai, was a pale gold color bordering on tan. Their offspring ran the full color range that can be seen today. There were parti-colored dogs in black and white, grizzle and white, and brown and white. There were solids in gold and honey color.

Shortly after sending the first pair of Lhasa Apsos, the Dalai Lama sent three more. These were followed a few years later, when the Cuttings were guests in the Potala Palace, by a pair that were bright golden. The last pair was sent by the Fourteenth Dalai Lama to the Cuttings shortly after the end of World War II.

With these dogs imported directly from Tibet, the Cuttings established their world-famous kennel under the name of Hamilton Farms in Gladstone, New Jersey.

The Potala Palace in Lhasa, the capital of Tibet, was the traditional home of the Dalai Lama through the centuries.

Pillars of the Breed

There are many kennels that breed and show Lhasa Apsos today, and still others that were once prominent but are no longer operating. Trying to select a limited number for discussion will always mean omitting some that are most certainly worthy of being mentioned for having made significant contributions to the fame and popularity of the Lhasa Apso. Kennels discussed here have been selected to represent all parts of the country and will include those that have produced many champions as well as those that have produced relatively few champions. The listing of these kennels is in alphabetical order according to kennel prefix.

Al Mar Kennel of Mrs. Marjorie Lewis is located in Missouri. Mrs. Lewis has only recently started breeding and showing Lhasa Apsos. An all-breed professional handler for many years, she has finished dozens of Maltese champions under her Al-Mar Kennel prefix.

Mrs. Lewis purchased Orlane's Be Sparky of Al-Mar as a newly weaned puppy. This deep red male finished his championship easily and has been a regular Group winner since. He is the sire of Ch. Al-Mar's Ala-Kazam belonging to Mrs. Linda Bullard.

One of the early prominent kennels—America's Kennel—was owned by Mrs. Marie Stillman of California. Mrs. Stillman was most fortunate to obtain Hamilton Torma as a foundation bitch for her kennel. Torma was finished to her title by Mrs. Stillman and then campaigned. In 1957 Torma was Best of Breed at Westminster and placed second in the Group. In October of 1957 she made breed history by being the first Lhasa Apso to go Best in Show. She earned the award under All-Breed Judge Maurice Baker.

Ch. Hamilton Torma was the dam of several champions that made records of their own. Ch. America's Torma Lu, purchased by Mrs. Dorothy Benitz, won the breed at Westminster in 1965 and went on to place Fourth in the Group. A daughter, Ch. America's Rika, achieved fame as the dam of Ch. Licos Kulu La, the second Lhasa Apso to win Best in Show. Kulu La earned a total of five Best-in-Show awards, which stood for a number of years as the record in the breed. Mrs. Stillman's breeding program was established on the Hamilton Farms stock that she had obtained from the Cuttings in the early 1950s.

A young kennel, but one that has produced several Group and Best-in-Show winning Lhasa Apsos, is Arborhill's Kennel owned by Robert and Sharon Binkowski of Michigan. The homebred Best-in-Show Ch. Arborhill's Rapso-Dieh is the son of the all-time great sire and Best-in-Show winner Ch. Everglo's Spark of Gold. Rapso-Dieh was not only a great showman but also proved to be a fine stud dog. He sired the Best-in-Show Ch. Arborhill's Rah-Kieh, whose offspring are just now appearing in the ring and are establishing records of their own.

Bar-Con Kennel of Barry and Connie Tompkins in New York is one of the most recently established kennels today. The Tompkins' first litter of Lhasa Apsos produced Ch. Bar-Con's the Avenger. Avenger is the son of Ch. Everglo's Spark of Gold and is co-owned by Dorothy Kendall. He is a multiple all-breed Best-in-Show winner and won the Eastern Specialty of the American Lhasa Apso Club in 1973. A litter mate of Avenger is the bitch Ch. Bar-Con's Double Trouble. Another young dog from this kennel is Ch. Bar-Con's Averagus.

Berano's Kennel in Wisconsin is operated by Bea and Ralph Gutelius. This kennel has been active in the Midwest for more than a dozen years. One of its early winners was Ch. Maida Manor Sun Set. He was campaigned in the early 1960s and was a serious Group contender wherever he appeared. When he was retired, the Guteliuses brought out their homebred Ch. Berano's Little Princess. She was a flashy little parti-colored bitch and made many friends for the breed with her winning personality. Mr. Gutelius has recently become a professional handler and is now seen in the ring with numerous other breeds as well as the Lhasa Apso.

Mrs. Patricia Chenoweth is the owner of Chen Kennel in California. She has bred and shown a number of Lhasa Apsos to championship. She is the co-breeder, along with Frances Harwell, of the 1972 record holder of the breed, Ch. Chen Korum-Ti. Among other honors he has earned, this fine dog was the leading Lhasa Apso under the Phillips System for 1972 with 14,070 points. He was the winner of the Western ALAC Specialty in both 1971 and 1972 as well as the Eastern Specialty in 1972. In semi-retirement now, he can still be seen occasionally in the show ring.

Other dogs carrying the kennel name are Ch. Chen Omar Khayyam, Ch. Chen Tag-Ser of Shahi-Taj, and the bitches, Ch. Chen Kamala Nor and Ch. Chen Ti Kara of Karo-La.

Cherryshore's Kennel, located in the Midwest, has established an enviable record. Ch. Cherryshore's Bah Bieh Boi, with his bright orange-gold coat, has made many friends for the breed. He was campaigned during the late 1960s and achieved considerable Group recognition. He has proved himself as an outstanding producer and his name can be found in the pedigrees of many winning dogs today.

Mrs. Peggy Haas of Michigan has produced a number of champions under the Crest-O-Lake prefix. Her bitch Ch. Crest-O-Lake Pretti Plez has been the leading show bitch in the Midwest. She is always a serious contender for the breed. Pretti Plez was shown regularly by Mrs. Haas's daughter Karen, who was a consistent winner in Junior Showmanship.

Mrs. Diane Dansereau's Dandi Kennel in Louisiana is another new kennel that is establishing a record in the show ring. Ch. Dandi's Golden Nugget was joined in the ring by his kennel mate, Ch. Dandi's Wa-Hoo, who has added a Group win to her credit.

Darno Kennel in Illinois is owned by the Milehams. Ch. Luty Tony of Darno and Ch. Darno Lama headed their stud force. In addition to Lhasa Apsos, the Milehams also breed Cairns.

Mrs. Winifred E. Drake of Florida is the owner of Drax Kennels. Dogs carrying the Drax prefix have been consistent winners in the South. Several of these dogs were sired by the great producer Ch. Colarlie's Shan Bangalor. For several years he held the record as the leading sire in the history of the breed. His qualities are easily recognized in his offspring.

Dunklehaven Kennel in Ohio is owned by Mr. and Mrs. J. R. Dunkle. This comparatively new kennel has produced several champions and a number with points toward their championship. Their Specials dog, Ch. Neika's Pleasing Pal, co-owned with Leonard Parsons, is starting out on a promising Group career. A fine young bitch, Ch. Dunklehaven Bianca, was finished by her new owner, Mrs. Carroll A. Riddle of Ohio.

A tableful of champions owned by Mrs. John Licos, done up with ribbons to celebrate the Christmas Holidays. From left to right: Ch. Americal's Leng Kong (D), Ch. Americal's Rika (B), Ch. Hamilton Pluti (B), Ch. Licos Nyapso La (B), Ch. Hamilton Katha (B), Ch. Licos Kulu La (D), and Ch. Licos Karo La (B).

Ms. Barbara Garrison of Georgia has finished a number of flashy dogs under the Dzong Kennel name. Ch. Dzong Bamboo Pete, a Ch. Colarlie's Shan Bangalor son, was recognized for his substance and soundness. Ch. Dzong Firelight has sired several champions carrying the Dzong prefix.

Mrs. Gloria Fowler of California has influenced the breed significantly under her Everglo Kennel name. Her brood bitch Tibetan Cookie of Everglo, while never finishing to her title, was the dam of the leading sire in the history of the breed—Ch. Everglo's Spark of Gold. He was sold as a puppy along with his young kennel mate, Kai Sang's Flame of Everglo, to Mrs. Dorothy Kendall of Iowa, who finished both of these dogs. They became the foundation stock of her Orlane Kennels. Other fine champions from Everglo are: Ch. Everglo's Charlie Brown and Ch. Everglo Zijuh Tomba, who won Best of Breed at the Western ALAC Specialty in 1970.

Mr. and Mrs. Glen Bagley operated a small kennel in California. Ch. Shangri-La Rajan of Glen Pines was their foundation stud dog. Some of his winners are Ch. Glen Pine's Nanda Devi, Ch. Glen Pine's Ringka, and Ch. Joli Grumpa of Glen Pines.

Goodway Kennel of Texas has produced winning dogs carrying the kennel prefix—Ch. Goodway's Smokey Keepsake and Ch. Goodway's Chuho Lama.

The true patrons of the Lhasa Apso were Mr. and Mrs. C. Suydam Cutting, the original importers of the breed in the United States. This stock imported directly from Tibet is in the pedigree of almost every Lhasa Apso in the country today.

Ch. Sakya Kamaru, with Handler Dorothy Kendall and Judge William Fetner.

It is interesting to note that before Mr. Cutting took possession of Hamilton Farms Kennel, it was already a famous name in the dog world. Following World War I, J. C. Brady owned Hamilton Farms and ran it as a German Shepherd kennel. He imported and bred several of the top show winners of his day. His most famous dogs were Ch. Hamilton Erich von Grafenworth (D) and Ch. Hamilton Anni v. Humboldtpark (B). Both were German imports and were big winners in Europe before being imported by Brady.

The Cuttings were active breeders and exhibitors until the death of Mrs. Cutting in 1961, at which time Mr. Cutting sold his dogs to Mrs. Dorothy Cohen, who continues his breeding line under the name of Karma Kennel in Nevada. Mr. Cutting died in 1972.

Seen frequently in the ring in the early 1950s was Ch. Hamilton Tatsienlu. He not only enjoyed a fine career in the ring but also for

Ch. Maytime Jingle Belles
with Breeder-
Owner-Handler
Jack Slade.

Ch. Lui Gi's Shigatzoo with Handler Tom Kilcullen, Judge Theodore Wurmser, and International Ch. San Saba's Chi Chi Jimi with Handler Edna Voyles.

several years had the honor of being the top producing stud dog in the country. His name appears in more of the early pedigrees than almost any other name. His son Ch. Hamilton Achok was also a leading stud dog with a significant number of champions to his credit.

Ch. Hamilton Droma brought new recognition and interest to the breed with her wins in the early 1960s. Her graceful movement and her beautiful coat caught the eye of many judges. Ch. Hamilton Kalon and his son Ch. Hamilton Jimpa each sired several winning dogs. Kalon is another Tatsienlu son. Ch. Hamilton Karma proved herself in the ring and also as a top brood bitch, for she is the dam of several outstanding champions. Ch. Hamilton Sandupa, another Tatsienlu son, is responsible for several champion offspring.

There have been many other dogs and bitches that were pure Hamilton in breeding but carried other kennel prefixes and finished their championship. The honor for their wins in the show ring belongs not only to their owners, but also to the Cuttings, who established the line that they were to continue. The breeders of today are truly fortunate that someone with the interest and the financial resources of the Cuttings became interested in the Lhasa Apso. Without this dedicated sponsorship, the breed would undoubtedly not enjoy the recognition it has today.

Jerec Kennel of Mrs. Joan Ditton was originally established in Florida but was later moved to Missouri. Mrs. Ditton's leading stud dog is Ch. Potala Kinderland's Goliath. Bitches that carried the kennel name and acquired the championship title are Ch. Jerec's Char-La Wa and Ch. Jerec's Lho-Ra of Al-Mar.

Mrs. Dorothy Cohen of Nevada purchased all the stock of Hamilton Farms from Mr. Cutting in 1961. Mrs. Cohen not only finished a number of these dogs carrying the Hamilton prefix, but also bred and finished many of her own champions under the Karma title.

One of the big winners with the Karma prefix was Ch. Karma Frosty Knight O Everglo. He earned a number of Best-in-Show awards before being retired by his owners, Ms. Maria B. Aspuru and Ms. A. O. Rossie. While at public stud he produced a number of champion get.

Ch. Karma Kushog, a proven stud, was a serious breed contender.

Ch. Kam Bu Kyimo Tessa with Handler Norman Patton and Judge Mildred Heald.

Ch. San Saba's Chosen Lee-Sa with Handler Edna Voyles and Judge R. Schulte.

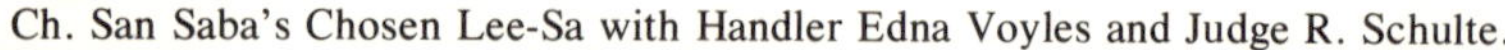

His clear light gold attracted much interest among breeders. He was able to pass on this quality to his offspring. The Karma and Americal lines united to produce such winners as Ch. Karma Naropa and Ch. Karma Pempa. Ch. Karma Rus-Ti, a dark orange, has done some great winning on the West Coast. He has proved his worth not only in the ring but also as a quality stud dog. He is the sire of many champions carrying the Karma Rus prefix, as well as several others.

Mrs. Cohen acquired Ch. Hamilton Tatsienlu when he was past his prime as a stud dog. He was still active for a number of years and able to get around until he was well into his teens. In recent years Mrs. Cohen has cut back on her breeding and showing program, but many of her dogs still appear in the pedigrees of leading winners today.

Mrs. Keke Blumberg established her Potala Kennel in Pennsylvania. The original prefix of "Keke's" has since been modified as "Potala Keke's." Three early winning and producing bitches are Ch. Keke's T'Chin T'Chin, her daughter Ch. Keke's T'Chin Ting T'Chin, and her granddaughter Ch. Keke's Bamboo.

Under the Potala prefix are several dogs that are winning currently. In the East is Ch. Potala Keke's Tomba Tu, owned by Mrs. Blumberg. In the Midwest is Ch. Potala Kinderland's Goliath, owned by Jerec Kennels.

The Kinderland Kennel of Mrs. Ellen Lonigro was first established in Missouri but was later moved to New Jersey. Mrs. Lonigro's first Specials dog was Ch. Larrmar De-Tsen, a son of Ch. Licos Kulu La. This huge-coated dog was a consistent breed winner in the Midwest and is the sire of numerous champions. Ch. Kinderland's Tonka, owned by Mr. and Mrs. Norman Herbel, is an all-breed Best-in-Show winner and was the Best-of-Opposite-Sex winner at the Western ALAC Specialty in 1972.

Ch. Kinderland's Sang-Po is the dam of many champions. Bred to several different studs, she has been a consistent producer of champions. A recent acquisition of Kinderland Kennels as a top producing stud dog is Ch. Ruffway Marpa.

Kyi-Chu Kennel in the Midwest combined the Hamilton and Colarlie breeding lines in their foundation stock. Ch. Quetzal Feyla of Kyi-Chi (bred by Mrs. J. Ammans and Ruth Smith and finished to his title by Dr. Robert J. Berndt) was bred back to his dam, Ch.

Ch. Miradel's Nima is an outstanding example of a parti-color.

Head study of Ch. Darno Be Mieh of Maraja.

Ch. Yum Yum Chu Chu of Strathmoore with Handler Edna Voyles and Judge Jean Lepley.

Ch. Maytime Genghis Khan with Owner-Handler Randy Gemmill and Judge C. L. Savage.

Colarlie's Miss Shandha, to produce an all-champion litter. The male in this litter was purchased by Mr. Robert Sharp. Mr. Sharp not only finished Kye-Chu Friar Tuck but also campaigned him to break the previous record by winning thirteen Best-in-Show awards. Friar Tuck won Best of Breed at the Eastern ALAC Specialty in 1968 and again in 1970. A daughter of Feyla, Ch. Orlane's Good as Gold, bred by Dorothy Kendall, also went on to win the coveted Best-in-Show ribbon.

Other winners under the Kyi-Chu title are: Ch. Kyi-Chu Whimsi of Sharbet and Ch. Kyi-Chu Yum Yum. Ch. Kyi-Chu Shara was Best of Breed at the Eastern ALAC Specialty in 1967.

Mrs. Grace Licos of California has bred many champions under the Licos prefix. Her big winner of the 1960s was Ch. Licos Kulu La. He was the second Lhasa Apso to win a Best-in-Show award. He later added four more top awards to his record. Ch. Licos Nyapso La was a full sister of Kulu La and another fine specimen of the breed. Ch. Licos Chulung La, a Nyapso son and the sire of fourteen champions, won the Veteran's Class at the Western ALAC Specialty in 1970.

Ch. Licos Omorfo La is a heavily coated golden son of Kulu La and established a winning record on the West Coast. He has passed on his winning qualities to his champion offspring. Mrs. Licos is still active in both breeding and showing in the West.

Lui-Gi's Kennel of Mrs. A. McFadden in Nevada produced a number of champions during the 1960s. Their leading sire was Ch. Lui-Gi's Shigatzoo, who was a son of Ch. Hamilton Jimpa.

Luty Kennel was established in Texas but was later moved to Illinois. Luty Kennel produced Ch. Luty Tony of Darno, Ch. Luty Buster, and Ch. Luty Mary Maude.

Jane and Raymond Bunse of Missouri have been breeding winning Lhasa Apsos under their kennel name of Maraja for a dozen years. Their homebred Ch. Maraja Tsering Momo was another of the early Best-in-Show winners. He and Ch. Maraja Ming Ti of Emberheights and Ch. Maraja Dolpho Karmo are the offspring of Ch. Ruffway Tsong Kapa.

Mrs. Rena Martin of Martin's Kennel in Illinois finished four champions from her foundation bitch, Ch. Karma Cricket Puff. A golden son, Ch. Martin's Kiwi Puff, and a black son, Ch. Martin's

Ch. Annie's Golden Fluff
with Handler Michael
Kemp.

Ch. Orlane's Sammie Jo
with Breeder-Handler
Dorothy Kendall.

Koala Puff, both went on to be Group winners. Mrs. Martin, who has also finished numerous Maltese champions, is now a professional handler.

Jack and Dorothy Slade of Indiana started their Maytime Kennel with Cocker Spaniels, finishing several champions before switching to Lhasa Apsos. In a short period of time they have bred and finished a number of champions. They acquired their foundation bitches from Mrs. Peggy Hogg of Illinois, who showed under the Morgantown title. The Slades did not "Special" any of their dogs and their record rests on their class wins. Their stud dog, Ch. Maytime Smoke O'Makulu, is carrying on their kennel line.

Milbryan Kennel in the South has crossed some of the leading bloodlines to produce their Ch. Milbryan Licos Gayla La and Ch. Milbryan Karma Vegas.

The Miradel Kennel of Eloris and L. R. Liebmann in California has produced champions that not only were outstanding in conformation but also were tops in obedience as well. Ch. Ming Tali II, C.D., was the foundation stud for the kennel and his name appears in nearly all Miradel pedigrees. Parti-colored winners from this kennel are Ch. Miradel's Nima, owned by Florence Bagley of California, and Ch. Miradel's Hsien Seng Chile, owned by Miss Jayne Berman of New York.

Mrs. Peggy Hogg, a professional handler, bred Lhasa Apsos in her Morgantown Kennel in Illinois for a few years. Two winners carrying the kennel name are Ch. Morgantown's Bob-O-Louie and Ch. Morgantown's Golden Boy.

Mrs. Phyllis Marcy of New Hampshire is the owner of Norbulingka Kennel. Her Ch. Kham of Norbulingka set the standard for winning for several years with his five Best-in-Show awards. Kham was Best of Breed at Westminster in 1966 and 1967 and was Best of Breed at the Eastern ALAC Specialty in 1966. This beautiful golden dog has left his stamp on many generations of winners. Ch. Lingkhor Bhu of Norbulingka, a Kham son, completed his championship at Westminster in 1971 and won Best of Breed at the same show in 1973.

Mrs. Dorothy Joan Kendall, a professional handler, is the owner of Orlane's Kennel in Iowa. Mrs. Kendall started out in Miniature Schnauzers before adding Lhasa Apsos more than a decade ago.

Ch. Shangri-La Rajan of
Glenn's Pines.

Ch. Arborhill's Bhran
Dieh with Handler
Maurine Peach and Judge
Mrs. Carl Cass.

Her foundation stud, Everglo's Spark of Gold, was purchased when he was three months old. Sparky became a champion and went on to win two Best-in-Show awards. He not only has proved to be a great showman, but also has become the leading sire in the history of the breed, with more than forty champion offspring and many others with major points. At the age of eleven he won the Veteran's Class at the Eastern ALAC Specialty in 1973 and was also winner of the Stud Dog Class. Some of Sparky's winning offspring are: Ch. Orlane's Dulmo, owned by Mrs. Irene Smith of Yat-Sen Kennel in Kentucky; Ch. Orlane's Gold Shipper, belonging to Mr. Ron Conner of Iowa; American, French, Belgian, Dutch, German, and Austrian Ch. Orlane's Golden Puppet; and Ch. Bar-Con's the Avenger.

Orlane's foundation bitch was Ch. Kai Sang's Flame of Everglo. In addition to being the dam of Puppet, she is also the dam of Ch. Orlane's Good as Gold, the Best-in-Show Bitch. Ch. Orlane's Oji-Hu was a litter mate of Puppet and Good as Gold. These dogs are half brothers and sisters of the famous Ch. Kyi-Chu Friar Tuck—all being offspring of Ch. Quetzal Feyal of Kyi-Chu.

Ch. Orlane Chitra of Ruffway, a Ch. Karma Frosty Knight O Everglo daughter, was the dam of an all-champion litter of five.

Pandan Kennel of California is owned by Mr. and Mrs. Robert Martin. Their foundation stud, Ch. Zijuh Seng-Tru, of pure Hamilton breeding, is the sire of seventeen champions. In addition to Ch. Pandan Choshe and Ch. Pandan Sheng Trou Cheng, who carry the kennel prefix, the following offspring have made strong wins in the East: Ch. Tabu's Kiss Me Kate, Ch. Potala Keke's Zin Zin, and American and Canadian Ch. Potala Keke's Yum Yum.

Jay Amann established her Quetzal Kennel of Skye Terriers in Oklahoma. She added Lhasa Apsos and changed the kennel prefix to Quizas. In addition to Ch. Quetzal Feyla of Kyi-Chu, Mrs. Amann has bred Ch. Quizas Shanzzi and Ch. Quizas Miranzzi.

Robert and Georgia Palmer have operated their Ruffway Kennel in Illinois for more than a dozen years. They have produced many champions and have earned many Group and Best-in-Show awards. Their homebred Ch. Ruffway Mashaka is a multiple Best-in-Show winner. This bright golden male is a superb example of the Standard of the Breed. Mashaka and his half brother Ch. Ruffway

Ch. SharBo Top Guy won a Best in Show from the Classes.

Ch. Everglo Spark of Gold, at eleven years of age, with his owner-handler, Dorothy Kendall.

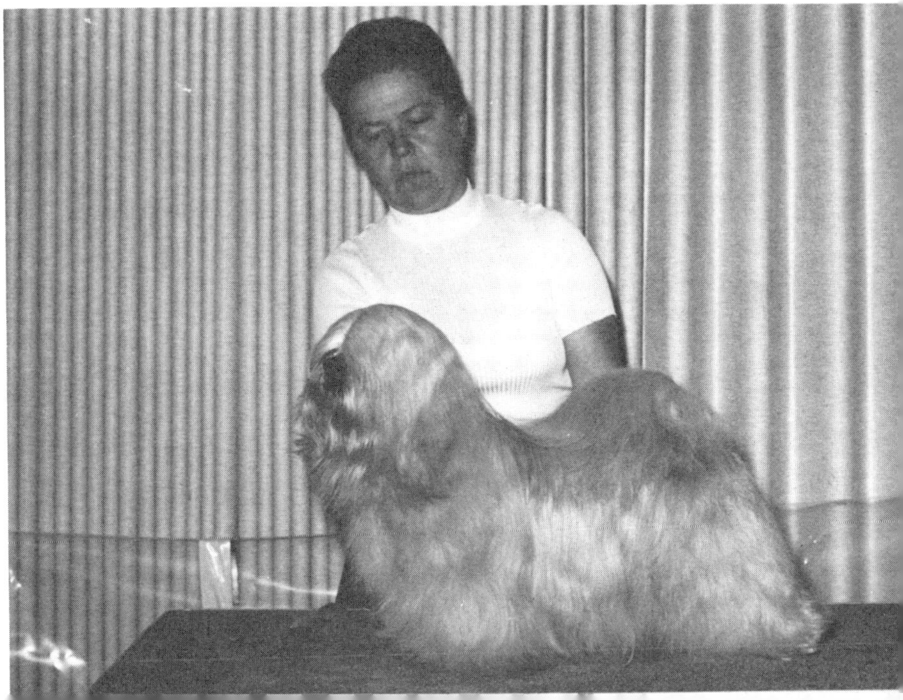

Marpa, owned by Ellen Lonigro of Kinderland Kennel, were both sired by Ch. Everglo's Spark of Gold.

The Palmers' early champions—Ch. Ruffway Tsong Kapa, Ch. Ruffway Solitaire, and Ch. Ruffway Neland—were from the Miradel line. With only limited showing, this small kennel has produced many outstanding dogs.

Mrs. Gail Maxwell of Texas established her Sakya Kennel in the 1960's. Her quality golden male, Ch. Sakya Kamaru, has been acquired by Bonneford Farms of Mrs. Donna Baxley of Maryland. Ch. Sakya Top Drawer and Ch. Sakya Mila are other young dogs from this kennel.

The San Saba Kennel, located in Texas, bred and finished a number of champions in the mid 1960s but has since ceased to exist as a Lhasa Apso kennel. Such winners as Ch. San Saba's Chosen Tiki Tu, Ch. San Saba Lhotse, Ch. San Saba Lori, and Ch. San Saba Tashi were all sired by the foundation stud, Ch. Lui-Gi's Shigatzoo. Most of the stock from this kennel was acquired by Mrs. Edna Voyles of Kentucky for her Cho Sen Vista Kennel.

In the late 1950s and into the 1960s, Mrs. Marilyn Sorci operated Shangri-La Kennel in California. Her Ch. Shangri-La Sho George and Ch. Shangri-La Rajan of Glen Pines, owned by the Glen Bagleys of California, were good examples of the rich gold of the Lhasa Apso. Mrs. Sorci's breeding stock was pure Hamilton through Ch. Hamilton Achok, one of the winning sons of Ch. Hamilton Tatsienlu. Mrs. Sorci's Ch. Hamilton Droma was the top winning Lhasa Apso in the country in 1964.

SharBo Kennel of Mrs. Sharon Rouse is located in California. This kennel has bred a number of dogs that are winning in the West. The foundation stud, Ch. Everglo Zijuh Tomba, is the sire of Ch. SharBo Zijuh Kamaru, a beautiful platinum gold owned by Mr. and Mrs. Richard McSorley of Rumtek Kennel in California. The Best-in-Show winning Ch. Sharbo Topguy is also owned by the McSorleys. Other SharBo winners of Mrs. Rouse are Ch. Sharbo Zijuh Zer Khan and Ch. SharBo Zijuh Esa Chu.

Sharpette's Kennel is located in New York and is owned by professional handler Robert Sharp and his wife, Jeanette. Their foundation stud was the record setting American, Canadian, Bermudian, and Mexican Ch. Kyi-Chu Friar Tuck. He earned thirteen Best-in-

Multiple Best-in-Show winner Ch. Kham of Norbulingka is owned by Phyllis Marcy
and was shown by Jane Kay.

Group winning Ch. Sharbo Zijuh Kamaru, owned by Richard and Darby McSorley.

Show awards and also took the Best-of-Breed prize at the Eastern ALAC Specialty in 1968 and again in 1970. He is proving himself as a leading sire with more than a dozen champion offspring.

Some of the winners under the Sharpette prefix are Ch. Sharpette's Galahad and Ch. Sharpette's Bobette, owned by Xanadu Kennel of Mr. and Mrs. David Goldfarb of New York. Ch. Sharpette's Number One Son and Ch. Sharpette's Lady Godiva are owned by Mr. and Mrs. Murray Teitelbaum of California. The Sharps have kept for their own kennel Ch. Sharpette's Cicero and Ch. Sharpette's Maha Maha.

Sherpa Kennel is owned by Clark and Kathy Pardon and is located in Michigan. While still a comparatively new kennel, Sherpa dogs are seen regularly in the show ring. The Pardon's foundation stud, Ch. Sherpa, is a silver gray. His young black daughter Ch. Sherpa's I'm A Pistol is already a multiple Group winner. In addition to Lhasa Apsos, the Pardons raise Shih Tzus. Mrs. Pardon has recently received her license to handle dogs professionally.

Mr. and Mrs. Norman Herbel acquired Ch. Tibet of Cornwallis as a stud and show dog for their Tabu Kennel in Pennsylvania. Tibet, a Best-in-Show winner, is the sire of Bermudian, Canadian, and American Ch. Kinderland's Tonka, who has won three Best-in-Show awards. The third Best-in-Show winner in this kennel is Bermudian, Canadian, and American Ch. Ku-Ka-Boh of Pickwick, who was also Best of Breed at the Eastern ALAC Specialty in 1969.

Among those dogs which have obtained championship titles under the Tabu prefix are: Ch. Tabu's Kiss Me Kate, Ch. Tabu's King of Hearts, and Ch. Tabu's Rapsody in Red. There are other young dogs nearing championship which should boost the producing record of this kennel.

Mrs. Virginia Knocke of Illinois established her Wynisippi Kennel to breed Yorkshire Terriers. She started her breeding program in Lhasa Apsos with the Best-in-Show Ch. Arborhill's Rah-Kieh. A young son of Ch. Ruffway Mashaka finished his title as Ch. Wynsippi Wyntrick Shalreign.

Yat-Sen Kennel of Mrs. Irene Smith in Kentucky started with Cocker Spaniels. The Cockers were joined shortly by a line of top producing Pekingese. When Mrs. Smith decided to add Lhasa

Apsos to her kennel, she bought Ch. Orlane's Dulma, a Ch. Everglo's Spark of Gold son. Mrs. Smith's son Larry "Specialed" Dulmo briefly. Dulmo was retired, however, when Larry entered the Navy. Dulmo has sired sixteen champions with more on the way. A Dulmo son, Ch. Kai-Song's Tuff Stuff of Yat-Sen, owned by Leslie T. Whitlow of Kentucky, won the Non-Sporting Group at the International Kennel Club fall show in 1972. Other winners are Ch. Raymer's Golden Girl of Yat-Sen, Ch. Yat-Sen's Khana, and Ch. Yat-Sen's Hazel.

Zijuh Kennel is located in California and produced its first champions in the middle 1960s. Zijuh established its breeding line on Hamilton and Everglo stock. Ch. Zijuh el Toro is by Ch. Karma Frosty Knight O Everglo, and Ch. Zijuh Tsam and Ch. Zijuh Kata are out of Ch. Hamilton Shim-Tru. Zijuh bloodlines have influenced the breeding programs of many California kennels.

A head study of Ch. Bar Con's the Avenger.

Am. and Can. Ch. Reiniet's St. Nicholas winning the Terrier Group in Canada.

Am. and Can. Ch. Caprice's Tsan Tse with Owner-Handler Peggy Hogg and Judge Joseph Faigel.

The Lhasa Apso in Other Countries

Although the Lhasa Apso had been exhibited in England for a number of years prior to that time, the breed did not achieve championship status there until 1965. Before a breed can achieve this status, the Kennel Club of Great Britain requires that 150 dogs per year must be registered over a three year period. The Lhasa Apso Club finally fulfilled this requirement and the first Challenge Certificates were awarded in 1965. Registrations not only have been maintained easily but also have increased greatly since then. The following registration figures indicate the increasing interest in the breed in Great Britain: 1965—160; 1966—180; 1967—208; 1968—239; 1969—346; 1970—404; 1971—563.

The first Lhasa Apso to attain an English championship was Brackenbury Gunga Din of Verles. He won five C.C.'s in succession and was then retired until the Cruft's Show in 1967, where he won his sixth C.C. and was awarded Best of Breed. He had previously won Best of Breed at Cruft's in 1963. He was shown by his owner, Mrs. Daphne M. Hesketh-Williams, who is Honorary Secretary of the Lhasa Apso Club of Great Britain. Ch. Brackenbury Gunga Din of Verles was bred by Miss Beryl Harding and sired by Jigmey Tharkay of Rungit, a dog imported from Tibet by Mrs. Jill Henderson.

The Lhasa Apso Club held its first breed specialty Open Show in March of 1969. Ninety-one entries were exhibited for Monsieur André Clement-Cuny, the French breeder who served as judge for the show. This Open Show has become a tradition and one is held each year in March. In 1970 the Lhasa Apso Club sponsored its first Championship Show. This show is also an annual event and is held in September. There are twenty classes and a Parade of Champions, and entries number about one hundred. The Lhasa Apso Club lists the Queen of Sikkim as one of its patrons.

The Lhasa Apso is shown in Great Britain in the Utility Group, which corresponds to the Non-Sporting Group in the United States.

Championship is attained in England by winning three Challenge Certificates. Since these certificates are not awarded at all shows, it is more difficult to attain the title of champion in England. In the first eight years since the breed's recognition, for example, there have been only thirty-two certificates of championship awarded. This is less than the number of championships awarded in the United States in a single year.

One of the outstanding kennels in England today is Belazieth Kennel in Essex, which is owned by Mr. and Mrs. R. G. Richardson. Their leading stud dog is Ch. Hardacre Hitchcock of Belazieth, who has earned nine Challenge Certificates and twenty-two Best-in-Show awards. In 1972 he won the Brackenbury Lhotse Points Cup for his outstanding record. His kennel mate, Ch. Belazieth's Honey Amber (B), has also won nine Challenge Certificates.

Mr. Paul Stanton of Wiltshire is the owner of Tintavon Kennels. His bitch Ch. Witcherty Thea of Tintavon won a Challenge Certificate at Cruft's in 1973.

Mrs. Anne Matthews of Sussex is the owner of Hardacre Kennels and the breeder of many winning Lhasa Apsos. Her homebred bitch Ch. Hardacre Hedda has won five Challenge Certificates, one of which was awarded at the Cruft's show in 1972.

The winner of the Challenge Certificates in dogs at the Cruft's show in 1973 was Ch. Cheska Alexander of Sternroc. He also went on to win Best of Breed at the same show. He was bred by Mrs. Frances F. Sefton on Cheska Kennel fame, and is co-owned by his breeder and Mrs. P. Cross Stern, whose Sternroc Kennel is located in Worcestershire. Alexander has earned fourteen Challenge Certificates. He is by Ch. Tayung of Coburg out of Ch. Cheska Bobette.

Mrs. Sefton is the author of *The Lhasa Apso*, which was published in England. She has since moved to Australia, where she continues to breed and show her dogs under the Cheska title. Her English Ch. Cheska Jesta now has her Australian Championship as well. Ch. Cheska Gregor, who earned eight Challenge Certificates, is also a Best-in-Show winner.

There are a number of other show kennels in England sharing the honor for advancing interest in the breed. Among these dedicated breeders are: Mrs. Irene Ashfield, Kobe Kennels, Kent; Mr. and Mrs. David Bluth, Saxonsprings Kennels, Yorkshire; and Miss Stephanie Hunt-Crowley, Chandhara Kennels, Buckingham.

Mr. Paul Stanton is the breeder of Tintavon Basieren, a young winning dog sold for export to Mrs. Lake of New Zealand. He is being campaigned in England before going to his new home. Tintavon Burundai, a Best-in-Show winner also bred by Mr. Stanton, has been exported to Miss Marina Ruetersward of Sweden.

Other Lhasa Apso breeders in Europe are: Mrs. Marianne Baurne of Sweden; Mlle. Dupont of Annapurna Kennels of France; Frau Nonc of Germany; and Mr. and Mrs. Anderson of Denmark.

Dorothy Kendall of Orlane Kennels in Burlington, Iowa, exported her Ch. Orlane's Golden Puppet to Mrs. Mewis Van Der Ruck of Belgium. Puppet completed championships in Belgium, Germany, France, Austria, and Holland and also earned the title of *Bundessieger* in Germany before he was returned to the United States. He has left a number of champion offspring in Europe.

In Canada the Lhasa Apso is shown in the Terrier Group. While there may be justification for this classification, it does not seem to be the best place to show this breed. The temperament of the Lhasa Apso is just a little too serene in comparison to that of other Terriers. The dog will not spar as a Terrier is expected to, and, therefore, does not show to his full advantage. To earn the title of champion in Canada a dog needs only ten points. It is possible to earn a championship point without meeting competition in the breed. Many breeders feel, therefore, that the title of champion in Canada means less than the title of champion does in the United States.

Mr. and Mrs. James Roberts are the owners of Abbotsford Kennels in British Columbia. They have finished a number of international champions during the past years. One of their leading winners is American and Canadian Ch. Teako of Abbotsford, who won the Western LACA Specialty in 1969. He is by the English dog Brackenbury Kandron out of American and Canadian Ch. Kalula of Abbotsford.

Dr. Ellen Brown, whose Balrene Kennel is located in Ontario, has also established an enviable show record for her dogs. Her American and Canadian Ch. Balrene Chia Pao, a consistent Group

Am. and Can. Ch.
Keepsake as a
four-month-old puppy.

winner, won Best-in-Show at the Specialty of the Lhasa Apso Club
of America held in Trenton, New Jersey, in 1971.

A winner of a few years back is the American and Canadian Ch.
Keepsake. He was bred by Maureen Crozier and Jasmin Bellany of
Calgary and shown to his Canadian championship by Miss Crozier.
He was finished to his American title by his owner, Dr. Robert J.
Berndt. His half sister, American and Canadian Ch. Caprice's Tsan
Te, was also finished by Miss Crozier in Canada and by her owner,
Peggy Hogg, in the United States.

Am. and Can. Ch.
Keepsake groomed and
ready for the ring.

Manners for
the Family Dog

Although each dog has personality quirks and idiosyncrasies that set him apart as an individual, dogs in general have two characteristics that can be utilized to advantage in training. The first is the dog's strong desire to please, which has been built up through centuries of association with man. The second lies in the innate quality of the dog's mentality. It has been proved conclusively that while dogs have reasoning power, their learning ability is based on a direct association of cause and effect, so that they willingly repeat acts that bring pleasant results and discontinue acts that bring unpleasant results. Hence, to take fullest advantage of a dog's abilities, the trainer must make sure the dog understands a command, and then reward him when he obeys and correct him when he does wrong.

Commands should be as short as possible and should be repeated in the same way, day after day. Saying "Heel," one day, and "Come here and heel," the next will confuse the dog. *Heel, sit, stand, stay, down,* and *come* are standard terminology, and are preferable for a dog that may later be given advanced training.

Tone of voice is important, too. For instance, a coaxing tone helps cajole a young puppy into trying something new. Once an exercise is mastered, commands given in a firm, matter-of-fact voice give the dog confidence in his own ability. Praise, expressed in an exuberant tone will tell the dog quite clearly that he has earned his master's approval. On the other hand, a firm "No" indicates with equal clarity that he has done wrong.

Rewards for good performance may consist simply of praising lavishly and petting the dog, although many professional trainers use bits of food as rewards. Tidbits are effective only if the dog is hungry, of course. And if you smoke, you must be sure to wash your hands before each training session, for the odor of nicotine is repulsive to dogs. On the hands of a heavy smoker, the odor of nicotine may be so strong that the dog is unable to smell the tidbit.

Correction for wrong-doing should be limited to repeating "No," in a scolding tone of voice or to confining the dog to his bed. Spanking or striking the dog is taboo—particularly using sticks, which might cause injury, but the hand should never be used either. For field training as well as some obedience work, the hand is used to signal the dog. Dogs that have been punished by slapping have a tendency to cringe whenever they see a hand raised and consequently do not respond promptly when the owner's intent is not to punish but to signal.

Some trainers recommend correcting the dog by whacking him with a rolled-up newspaper. The idea is that the newspaper will not injure the dog but that the resulting noise will condition the dog to avoid repeating the act that seemingly caused the noise. Many authorities object to this type of correction, for it may result in the dog's becoming "noise-shy"—a decided disadvantage with show dogs which must maintain poise in adverse, often noisy, situations. "Noise-shyness" is also an unfortunate reaction in field dogs, since it may lead to gun-shyness.

To be effective, correction must be administered immediately, so that in the dog's mind there is a direct connection between his act and the correction. You can make voice corrections under almost any circumstances, but you must never call the dog to you and then correct him, or he will associate the correction with the fact that he has come and will become reluctant to respond. If the dog is at a distance and doing something he shouldn't, go to him and scold him while he is still involved in wrong-doing. If this is impossible, ignore the offense until he repeats it and you can correct him properly.

Especially while a dog is young, he should be watched closely and stopped before he gets into mischief. All dogs need to do a certain amount of chewing, so to prevent your puppy's chewing something you value, provide him with his own rubber balls and toys. Never allow him to chew cast-off slippers and then expect him to differentiate between cast-off items and those you value. Nylon stockings, wooden articles, and various other items may cause intestinal obstructions if the dog chews and swallows them, and death may result. So it is essential that the dog be permitted to chew only on bones or rubber toys.

Serious training for obedience should not be started until a dog is a year old. But basic training in house manners should begin the day the puppy enters his new home. A puppy should never be given the run of the house but should be confined to a box or small pen except for play periods when you can devote full attention to him. The first thing to teach the dog is his name, so that whenever he hears it, he will immediately come to attention. Whenever you are near his box, talk to him, using his name repeatedly. During play periods, talk to him, pet him, and handle him, for he must be conditioned so he will not object to being handled by a veterinarian, show judge, or family friend. As the dog investigates his surroundings, watch him carefully and if he tries something he shouldn't, reprimand him with a scolding "No!" If he repeats the offense, scold him and confine him to his box, then praise him. Discipline must be prompt, consistent, and always followed with praise. Never tease the dog, and never allow others to do so. Kindness and understanding are essential to a pleasant, mutually rewarding relationship.

When the puppy is two to three months old, secure a flat, narrow leather collar and have him start wearing it (never use a harness, which will encourage tugging and pulling). After a week or so, attach a light leather lead to the collar during play sessions and let the puppy walk around, dragging the lead behind him. Then start holding the end of the lead and coaxing the puppy to come to you. He will then be fully accustomed to collar and lead when you start taking him outside while he is being housebroken.

Housebreaking can be accomplished in a matter of approximately two weeks provided you wait until the dog is mature enough to have some control over bodily functions. This is usually at about four months. Until that time, the puppy should spend most of his day confined to his penned area, with the floor covered with several thicknesses of newspapers so that he may relieve himself when necessary without damage to floors.

Either of two methods works well in housebreaking—the choice depending upon where you live. If you live in a house with a readily accessible yard, you will probably want to train the puppy from the beginning to go outdoors. If you live in an apartment without easy access to a yard, you may decide to train him first to relieve himself on newspapers and then when he has learned control, to teach the puppy to go outdoors.

If you decide to train the puppy by taking him outdoors, arrange some means of confining him indoors where you can watch him closely—in a small penned area, or tied to a short lead (five or six feet). Dogs are naturally clean animals, reluctant to soil their quarters, and confining the puppy to a limited area will encourage him to avoid making a mess.

A young puppy must be taken out often, so watch your puppy closely and if he indicates he is about to relieve himself, take him out at once. If he has an accident, scold him and take him out so he will associate the act of going outside with the need to relieve himself. Always take the puppy out within an hour after meals—preferably to the same place each time—and make sure he relieves himself before you return him to the house. Restrict his water for two hours before bedtime and take him out just before you retire for the night. Then, as soon as you wake in the morning, take him out again.

For paper training, set aside a particular room and cover a large area of the floor with several thicknesses of newspapers. Confine the dog on a short leash and each time he relieves himself, remove the soiled papers and replace them with clean ones.

As his control increases, gradually decrease the paper area, leaving part of the floor bare. If he uses the bare floor, scold him mildly and put him on the papers, letting him know that there is where he is to relieve himself. As he comes to understand the idea, increase the bare area until papers cover only space equal to approximately two full newspaper sheets. Keep him using the papers, but begin taking him on a leash to the street at the times of day that he habitually relieves himself. Watch him closely when he is indoors and at the first sign that he needs to go, take him outdoors. Restrict his water for two hours before bedtime, but if necessary, permit him to use the papers before you retire for the night.

Using either method, the puppy will be housebroken in an amazingly short time. Once he has learned control he will need to relieve himself only four or five times a day.

Informal obedience training, started at the age of about six to eight months, will provide a good background for any advanced training you may decide to give your dog later. The collar most

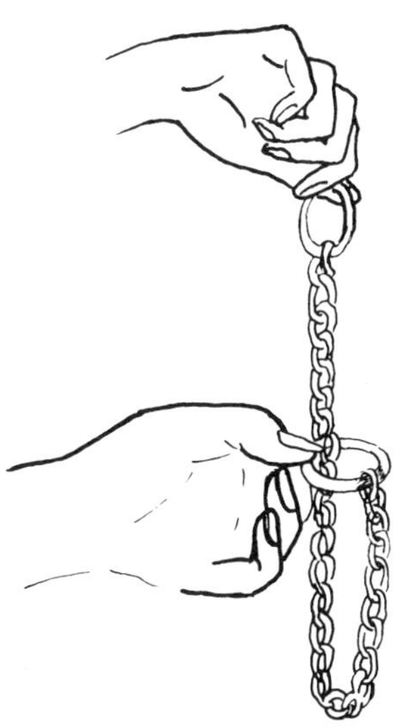

effective for training is the metal chain-link variety. The correct size for your dog will be about one inch longer than the measurement around the largest part of his head. The chain must be slipped through one of the rings so the collar forms a loop. The collar should be put on with the loose ring at the right of the dog's neck, the chain attached to it coming over the neck and through the holding ring, rather than under the neck. Since the dog is to be at your left during most of the training, this makes the collar most effective.

The leash should be attached to the loose ring, and should be either webbing or leather, six feet long and a half inch to a full inch wide. When you want your dog's attention, or wish to correct him, give a light, quick pull on the leash, which will momentarily tighten the collar about the neck. Release the pressure instantly, and the correction will have been made. If the puppy is already accustomed to a leather collar, he will adjust easily to the training collar. But before you start training sessions, practice walking with the dog until he responds readily when you increase tension on the leash.

Set aside a period of fifteen minutes, once or twice a day, for regular training sessions, and train in a place where there will be no distractions. Teach only one exercise at a time, making sure the dog has mastered it before going on to another. It will probably take at least a week for the dog to master each exercise. As training progresses, start each session by reviewing exercises the dog has already learned, then go on to the new exercise for a period of concerted practice. When discipline is required, make the correction immediately, and always praise the dog after corrections as well as when he obeys promptly. During each session stick strictly to business. Afterwards, take time to play with the dog.

The first exercise to teach is heeling. Have the dog at your left and hold the leash as shown in the illustration on the preceding page. Start walking, and just as you put your foot forward for the first step, say your dog's name to get his attention, followed by the command, "Heel!" Simultaneously, pull on the leash lightly. As you walk, try to keep the dog at your left side, with his head alongside your left leg. Pull on the leash as necessary to urge him forward or back, to right or left, but keep him in position. Each time you pull on the leash, say "Heel!" and praise the dog lavishly. When the dog heels properly in a straight line, start making circles, turning corners, etc.

Once the dog has learned to heel well, start teaching the "sit." Each time you stop while heeling, command "Sit!" The dog will be at your left, so use your left hand to press on his rear and guide him to a sitting position, while you use the leash in your right hand to keep his head up. Hold him in position for a few moments while you praise him, then give the command to heel. Walk a few steps, stop, and repeat the procedure. Before long he will automatically sit whenever you stop. You can then teach the dog to "sit" from any position.

When the dog will sit on command without correction, he is ready to learn to stay until you release him. Simply sit him, command "Stay!" and hold him in position for perhaps half a minute, repeating "Stay," if he attempts to stand. You can release him by saying "O.K." Gradually increase the time until he will stay on command for three or four minutes.

The "stand-stay" should also be taught when the dog is on leash. While you are heeling, stop and give the command "Stand!" Keep the dog from sitting by quickly placing your left arm under him, immediately in front of his right hind leg. If he continues to try to sit, don't scold him but start up again with the heel command, walk a few steps, and stop again, repeating the stand command and preventing the dog from sitting. Once the dog has mastered the stand, teach him to stay by holding him in position and repeating the word "Stay!"

The "down stay" will prove beneficial in many situations, but especially if you wish to take your dog in the car without confining him to a crate. To teach the "down," have the dog sitting at your side with collar and leash on. If he is a large dog, step forward with the leash in your hand and turn so you face him. Let the leash touch the floor, then step over it with your right foot so it is under the instep of your shoe. Grasping the leash low down with both hands, slowly pull up, saying, "Down!" Hold the leash taut until the dog goes down. Once he responds well, teach the dog to stay in the down position (the down-stay), using the same method as for the sit- and stand-stays.

To teach small dogs the "down," another method may be used. Have the dog sit at your side, then kneel beside him. Reach across his back with your left arm, and take hold of his left front leg close to the body. At the same time, with your right hand take hold of his right front leg close to his body. As you command "Down!" gently lift the legs and place the dog in the down position. Release your hold on his legs and slide your left hand onto his back, repeating, "Down, stay," while keeping him in position.

The "come" is taught when the dog is on leash and heeling. Simply walk along, then suddenly take a step backward, saying "Come!" Pull the leash as you give the command and the dog will turn and follow you. Continue walking backward, repeatedly saying "Come," and tightening the leash if necessary.

Once the dog has mastered the exercises while on leash, try taking the leash off and going through the same routine, beginning with the heeling exercise. If the dog doesn't respond promptly, he needs review with the leash on. But patience and persistence will be rewarded, for you will have a dog you can trust to respond promptly under all conditions.

Even after they are well trained, dogs sometimes develop bad habits that are hard to break. Jumping on people is a common habit, and all members of the family must assist if it is to be broken. If the dog is a large or medium breed, take a step forward and raise your knee just as he starts to jump on you. As your knee strikes the dog's chest, command "Down!" in a scolding voice. When a small dog jumps on you, take both front paws in your hands, and, while talking in a pleasant tone of voice, step on the dog's back feet just hard enough to hurt them slightly. With either method the dog is taken by surprise and doesn't associate the discomfort with the person causing it.

Occasionally a dog may be too chummy with guests who don't care for dogs. If the dog has had obedience training, simply command "Come!" When he responds, have him sit beside you.

Excessive barking is likely to bring complaints from neighbors, and persistent efforts may be needed to subdue a dog that barks without provocation. To correct the habit, you must be close to the dog when he starts barking. Encircle his muzzle with both hands, hold his mouth shut, and command "Quiet!" in a firm voice. He should soon learn to respond so you can control him simply by giving the command.

Sniffing other dogs is an annoying habit. If the dog is off leash and sniffs other dogs, ignoring your commands to come, he needs to review the lessons on basic behavior. When the dog is on leash, scold him, then pull on the leash, command "Heel," and walk away from the other dog.

A well-trained dog will be no problem if you decide to take him with you when you travel. No matter how well he responds, however, he should never be permitted off leash when you walk him in a strange area. Distractions will be more tempting, and there will be more chance of his being attacked by other dogs. So whenever the dog travels with you, take his collar and leash along— and use them.

Bench Shows

Centuries ago, it was common practice to hold agricultural fairs in conjunction with spring and fall religious festivals, and to these gatherings, cattle, dogs, and other livestock were brought for exchange. As time went on, it became customary to provide entertainment, too. Dogs often participated in such sporting events as bull baiting, bear baiting, and ratting. Then the dog that exhibited the greatest skill in the arena was also the one that brought the highest price when time came for barter or sale. Today, these fairs seem a far cry from our highly organized bench shows and field trials. But they were the forerunners of modern dog shows and played an important role in shaping the development of purebred dogs.

The first organized dog show was held at Newcastle, England, in 1859. Later that same year, a show was held at Birmingham. At both shows dogs were divided into four classes and only Pointers and Setters were entered. In 1860, the first dog show in Germany was held at Apoldo, where nearly one hundred dogs were exhibited and entries were divided into six groups. Interest expanded rapidly, and by the time the Paris Exhibition was held in 1878, the dog show was a fixture of international importance.

In the United States, the first organized bench show was held in 1874 in conjunction with the meeting of the Illinois State Sportsmen's Association in Chicago, and all entries were dogs of sporting breeds. Although the show was a rather casual affair, interest spread quickly. Before the end of the year, shows were held in Oswego, New York, Mineola, Long Island, and Memphis, Tennessee. And the latter combined a bench show with the first organized field trial ever held in the United States. In January 1875, an all-breed show (the first in the United States) was held at Detroit, Michigan. From then on, interest increased rapidly, though rules were not always uniform, for there was no organization through which to coordinate activities until September 1884

Benching area at Westminster Kennel Club Show.

Judging for Best in Show at Westminster Kennel Club Show.

when The American Kennel Club was founded. Now the largest dog registering organization in the world, the A.K.C. is an association of several hundred member clubs—all breed, specialty, field trial, and obedience groups—each represented by a delegate to the A.K.C.

The several thousand shows and trials held annually in the United States do much to stimulate interest in breeding to produce better looking, sounder, purebred dogs. For breeders, shows provide a means of measuring the merits of their work as compared with accomplishments of other breeders. For hundreds of thousands of dog fanciers, they provide an absorbing hobby.

For both spectators and participating owners, field trials constitute a fascinating demonstration of dogs competing under actual hunting conditions, where emphasis is on excellence of performance. The trials are sponsored by clubs or associations of persons interested in hunting dogs. Trials for Pointing breeds, Dachshunds, Retrievers, Spaniels, and Beagles are under the jurisdiction of The American Kennel Club and information concerning such activities is published in "Pure Bred Dogs—American Kennel Gazette." Trials for Bird Dogs are run by rules and regulations of the Amateur Field Trial Clubs of America and information concerning them is published in "The American Field."

All purebred dogs of recognized breeds may be registered with The American Kennel Club and those of hunting breeds may also be registered with The American Field. Dogs that have won championships both in the field and in bench shows are known as dual champions.

At bench (or conformation) shows, dogs are rated comparatively on their physical qualities (or conformation) in accordance with breed Standards which have been approved by The American Kennel Club. Characteristics such as size, coat, color, placement of eye or ear, general soundness, etc., are the basis for selecting the best dog in a class. Only purebred dogs are eligible to compete and if the show is one where points toward a championship are to be awarded, a dog must be at least six months old.

Bench shows are of various types. An all-breed show has classes for all of the breeds recognized by The American Kennel Club as well as a Miscellaneous Class for breeds not recognized, such as the Australian Cattle Dog, the Ibizan Hound, the Spinoni Italiani, the Tibetan Terrier, etc. A sanctioned match is an informal meeting where dogs compete but not for championship points. A specialty show is confined to a single breed. Other shows may restrict entries to champions of record, to American-bred dogs, etc. Competition for Junior Showmanship or for Best Brace, Best Team, or Best Local Dog may be included. Also, obedience competition is held in conjunction with many bench shows.

The term "bench show" is somewhat confusing in that shows of this type may be either "benched" or "unbenched." At the former, each dog is assigned an individual numbered stall where he must remain throughout the show except for times when he is being judged, groomed, or exercised. At unbenched shows, no stalls are provided and dogs are kept in their owners' cars or in crates when not being judged.

A show where a dog is judged for conformation actually constitutes an elimination contest. To begin with, the dogs of a single breed compete with others of their breed in one of the regular classes: Puppy, Novice, Bred by Exhibitor, American-Bred, or Open, and, finally, Winners, where the top dogs of the preceding five classes meet. The next step is the judging for Best of Breed (or Best of Variety of Breed). Here the Winners Dog and Winners Bitch (or the dog named Winners if only one prize is awarded) compete with any champions that are entered, together with any undefeated dogs that have competed in additional non-regular classes. The dog named Best of Breed (or Best of Variety of Breed), then goes on to compete with the other Best of Breed winners in his Group. The dogs that win in Group competition then compete for the final and highest honor, Best in Show.

When the Winners Class is divided by sex, championship points are awarded the Winners Dog and Winners Bitch. If the Winners Class is not divided by sex, championship points are awarded the dog or bitch named Winners. The number of points awarded varies, depending upon such factors as the number of dogs competing, the Schedule of Points established by the Board of Directors of the A.K.C., and whether the dog goes on to win Best of Breed, the Group, and Best in Show.

In order to become a champion, a dog must win fifteen points, including points from at least two major wins—that is, at least two shows where three or more points are awarded. The major wins must be under two different judges, and one or more of the remaining points must be won under a third judge. The most points ever awarded at a show is five and the least is one, so, in order to become

Junior Showmanship Competition at Westminster Kennel Club Show.

a champion, a dog must be exhibited and win in at least three shows, and usually he is shown many times before he wins his championship.

"Pure Bred Dogs—American Kennel Gazette" and other dog magazines contain lists of forthcoming shows, together with names and addresses of sponsoring organizations to which you may write for entry forms and information relative to fees, closing dates, etc. Before entering your dog in a show for the first time, you should familiarize yourself with the regulations and rules governing competition. You may secure such information from The American Kennel Club or from a local dog club specializing in your breed. It is essential that you also familiarize yourself with the A.K.C. approved Standard for your breed so you will be fully aware of characteristics worthy of merit as well as those considered faulty, or possibly even serious enough to disqualify the dog from competition. For instance, monorchidism (failure of one testicle to descend) and cryptorchidism (failure of both testicles to descend) are disqualifying faults in all breeds.

If possible, you should first attend a show as a spectator and observe judging procedures from ringside. It will also be helpful to join a local breed club and to participate in sanctioned matches before entering an all-breed show.

The dog should be equipped with a narrow leather show lead and a show collar—never an ornamented or spiked collar. For benched shows, a metal-link bench chain will be needed to fasten the dog to the bench. For unbenched shows, the dog's crate should be taken along so that he may be confined in comfort when he is not appearing in the ring. A dog should never be left in a car with all the windows closed. In hot weather the temperature will become unbearable in a very short time. Heat exhaustion may result from even a short period of confinement, and death may ensue.

Food and water dishes will be needed, as well as a supply of the food and water to which the dog is accustomed. Brushes and combs are also necessary, so that you may give the dog's coat a final grooming after you arrive at the show.

Familiarize yourself with the schedule of classes ahead of time, for the dog must be fed and exercised and permitted to relieve himself, and any last-minute grooming completed before his class is called. Both you and the dog should be ready to enter the ring unhurriedly. A good deal of skill in conditioning, training, and handling is required if a dog is to be presented properly. And it is essential that the handler himself be composed, for a jittery handler will transmit his nervousness to his dog.

Once the class is assembled in the ring, the judge will ask that the dogs be paraded in line, moving counter-clockwise in a circle. If you have trained your dog well, you will have no difficulty controlling him in the ring, where he must change pace quickly and gracefully and walk and trot elegantly and proudly with head erect. The show dog must also stand quietly for inspection, posing like a statue for several minutes while the judge observes his structure in detail, examines teeth, feet, coat, etc. When the judge calls your dog forward for individual inspection, do not attempt to converse, but answer any questions he may ask.

As the judge examines the class, he measures each dog against the ideal described in the Standard, then measures the dogs against each other in a comparative sense and selects for first place the dog that comes closest to conforming to the Standard for its breed. If your dog isn't among the winners, don't grumble. If he places first, don't brag loudly. For a bad loser is disgusting, but a poor winner is insufferable.

For hundreds of years, dogs have been used in England and Germany in connection with police and guard work, and their working potential has been evaluated through tests devised to show agility, strength, and courage. Organized training has also been popular with English and German breeders for many years, although it was first practiced primarily for the purpose of training large breeds in aggressive tactics.

There was little interest in obedience training in the United States until 1933 when Mrs. Whitehouse Walker returned from England and enthusiastically introduced the sport. Two years later, Mrs. Walker persuaded The American Kennel Club to approve organized obedience activities and to assume jurisdiction over obedience rules. Since then, interest has increased at a phenomenal rate, for obedience competition is not only a sport the average spectator can follow readily, but also a sport for which the average owner can train his own dog easily. Obedience competition is suitable for all breeds. Furthermore, there is no limit to the number of dogs that may win in competition, for each dog is scored individually on the basis of a point rating system.

The dog is judged on his response to certain commands, and if he gains a high enough score in three successive trials under different judges, he wins an obedience degree. Degrees awarded are "C.D."— Companion Dog; "C.D.X."—Companion Dog Excellent; and "U.D." —Utility Dog. A fourth degree, the "T.D.," or Tracking Dog degree, may be won at any time and tests for it are held apart from dog shows. The qualifying score is a minimum of 170 points out of a possible total of 200, with no score in any one exercise less than 50% of the points allotted.

Since obedience titles are progressive, earlier titles (with the exception of the tracking degree) are dropped as a dog acquires the next higher degree. If an obedience title is gained in another country in addition to the United States, that fact is signified by the word "International," followed by the title.

Trials for obedience trained dogs are held at most of the larger bench shows, and obedience training clubs are to be found in almost all communities today. Information concerning forthcoming trials and lists of obedience training clubs are included regularly in "Pure Bred Dogs—American Kennel Gazette"—and other dog magazines. Pamphlets containing rules and regulations governing obedience competition are available upon request from The American Kennel Club, 51 Madison Avenue, New York, N.Y. 10010. Rules are revised occasionally, so if you are interested in participating in obedience competition, you should be sure your copy of the regulations is current.

All dogs must comply with the same rules, although in broad jump, high jump, and bar jump competition, the jumps are adjusted to the size of the breed. Classes at obedience trials are divided into Novice (A and B), Open (A and B), and Utility (which may be divided into A and B, at the option of the sponsoring club and with the approval of The American Kennel Club).

The Novice class is for dogs that have not won the title Companion Dog. In Novice A, no person who has previously handled a dog that has won a C.D. title in the obedience ring at a licensed or member trial, and no person who has regularly trained such a dog, may enter or handle a dog. The handler must be the dog's owner or a member of the owner's immediate family. In Novice B, dogs may be handled by the owner or any other person.

The Open A class is for dogs that have won the C.D. title but have not won the C.D.X. title. Obedience judges and licensed handlers may not enter or handle dogs in this class. Each dog must be handled by the owner or by a member of his immediate family. The Open B class is for dogs that have won the title C.D. or C.D.X. A dog may continue to compete in this class after it has won the title U.D. Dogs in this class may be handled by the owner or any other person.

The Utility class is for dogs that have won the title C.D.X. Dogs that have won the title U.D. may continue to compete in this class, and dogs may be handled by the owner or any other person. Provided the A.K.C. approves, a club may choose to divide the Utility class into Utility A and Utility B. When this is done, the Utility A class is for dogs that have won the title C.D.X. and have not won the title U.D. Obedience judges and licensed handlers may not enter or handle dogs in this class. All other dogs that are eligible for the Utility class but not eligible for Utility A may be entered in Utility B.

Novice competition includes such exercises as heeling on and off lead, the stand for examination, coming on recall, and the long sit and the long down.

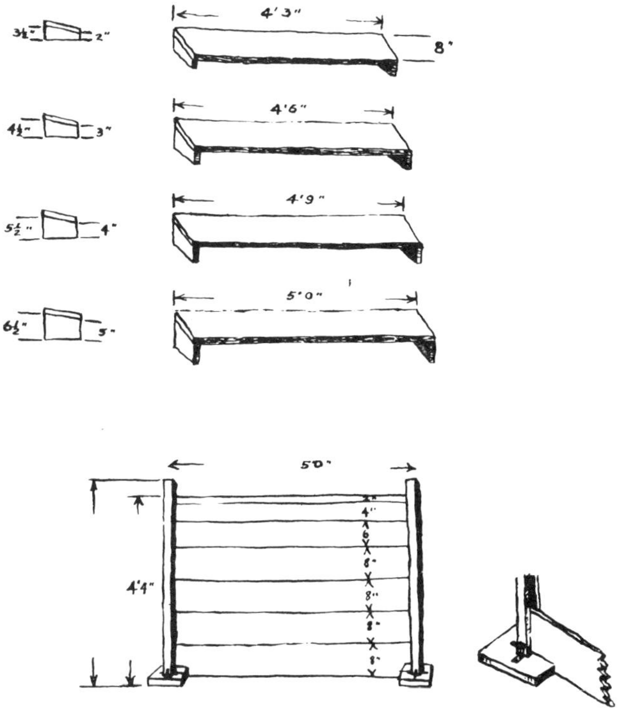

Broad jump and solid hurdle.

In Open competition, the dog must perform such exercises as heeling free, the drop on recall, and the retrieve on the flat and over the high jump. Also, he must execute the broad jump, and the long sit and long down.

In the Utility class, competition includes scent discrimination, the directed retrieve, the signal exercise, directed jumping, and the group examination.

Tracking is the most difficult test. It is always done out-of-doors, of course, and, for obvious reasons, cannot be held at a dog show. The dog must follow a scent trail that is about a quarter mile in length. He is also required to find a scent object (glove, wallet, or other article) left by a stranger who has walked the course to lay down the scent. The dog is required to follow the trail a half to two hours after the scent is laid.

An ideal way to train a dog for obedience competition is to join an obedience class or a training club. In organized class work, beginners' classes cover pretty much the same exercises as those

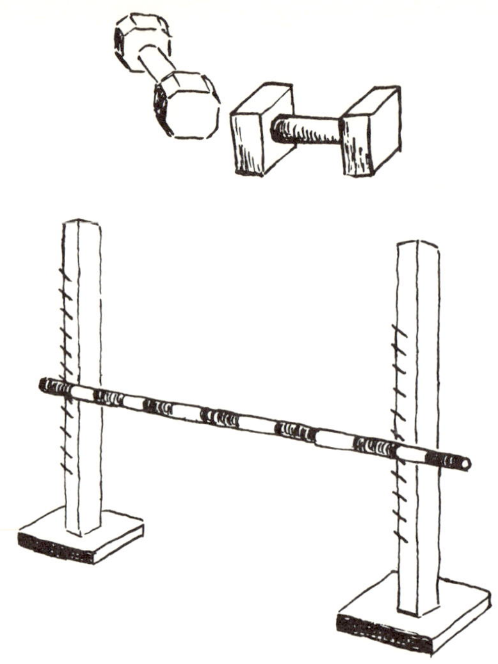

Dumbbells and bar jump.

described in the chapter on training. However, through class work you will develop greater precision than is possible in training your dog by yourself. Amateur handlers often cause the dog to be penalized, for if the handler fails to abide by the rules, it is the dog that suffers the penalty. A common infraction of the rules is using more than one signal or command where regulations stipulate only one may be used. Classwork will help eliminate such errors, which the owner may make unconsciously if he is working alone. Working with a class will also acquaint both dog and handler with ring procedure so that obedience trials will not present unforeseen problems.

Thirty or forty owners and dogs often comprise a class, and exercises are performed in unison, with individual instruction provided if it is required. The procedure followed in training—in fact, even wording of various commands—may vary from instructor to instructor. Equipment used will vary somewhat, also, but will usually include a training collar and leash such as those shown on page 109, a long line, a dumbbell, and a jumping stick.

The latter may be a short length of heavy doweling or a broom handle and both it and the dumbbell are usually painted white for increased visibility.

A bitch in season must never be taken to a training class, so before enrolling a female dog, you should determine whether she may be expected to come into season before classes are scheduled to end. If you think she will, it is better to wait and enroll her in a later course, rather than start the course and then miss classes for several weeks.

In addition to the time devoted to actual work in class, the dog must have regular, daily training sessions for practice at home. Before each class or home training session, the dog should be exercised so he will not be highly excited when the session starts, and he must be given an opportunity to relieve himself before the session begins. (Should he have an accident during the class, it is your responsibility to clean up after him.) The dog should be fed several hours before time for the class to begin or else after the class is over—never just before going to class.

If you decide to enter your dog in obedience competition, it is well to enter a small, informal show the first time. Dogs are usually called in the order in which their names appear in the catalog, so as soon as you arrive at the show, acquaint yourself with the schedule. If your dog is not the first to be judged, spend some time at ringside, observing the routine so you will know what to expect when your dog's turn comes.

In addition to collar, leash, and other equipment, you should take your dog's food and water pans and a supply of the food and water to which he is accustomed. You should also take his brushes and combs in order to give him a last-minute brushing before you enter the ring. It is important that the dog look his best even though he isn't to be judged on his appearance.

Before entering the ring, exercise your dog, give him a drink of water, and permit him to relieve himself. Once your dog enters the ring, give him your full attention and be sure to give voice commands distinctly so he will hear and understand, for there will be many distractions at ringside.

Top dogs in Utility Class. This illustrates variety of breeds that compete in obedience.

Genetics, the science of heredity, deals with the processes by which physical and mental traits of parents are transmitted to offspring. For centuries, man has been trying to solve these puzzles, but only in the last two hundred years has significant progress been made.

During the eighteenth century, Kölreuter, a German scientist, made revolutionary discoveries concerning plant sexuality and hybridization but was unable to explain just how hereditary processes worked. In the middle of the nineteenth century, Gregor Johann Mendel, an Augustinian monk, experimented with the ordinary garden pea and made other discoveries of major significance. He found that an inherited characteristic was inherited as a complete unit, and that certain characteristics predominated over others. Next, he observed that the hereditary characteristics of each parent are contained in each offspring, even when they are not visible, and that "hidden" characteristics can be transferred without change in their nature to the grandchildren, or even later generations. Finally, he concluded that although heredity contains an element of uncertainty, some things are predictable on the basis of well-defined mathematical laws.

Unfortunately, Mendel's published paper went unheeded, and when he died in 1884 he was still virtually unknown to the scientific world. But other researchers were making discoveries, too. In 1900, three different scientists reported to learned societies that much of their research in hereditary principles had been proved years before by Gregor Mendel and that findings matched perfectly.

Thus, hereditary traits were proved to be transmitted through the chromosomes found in pairs in every living being, one of each pair contributed by the mother, the other by the father. Within each chromosome have been found hundreds of smaller structures, or genes, which are the actual determinants of hereditary characteristics. Some genes are dominant and will be seen in the offspring. Others are recessive and will not be outwardly apparent, yet can be passed on to the offspring to combine with a similar recessive gene of the other parent and thus be seen. Or they may be passed on to the offspring, not be outwardly apparent, but be passed on again to become apparent in a later generation.

Once the genetic theory of inheritance became widely known, scientists began drawing a well-defined line between inheritance and environment. More recent studies show some overlapping of these influences and indicate a combination of the two may be responsible for certain characteristics. For instance, studies have proved that extreme cold increases the amount of black pigment in the skin and hair of the "Himalayan" rabbit, although it has little or no effect on the white or colored rabbit. Current research also indicates that even though characteristics are determined by the genes, some environmental stress occurring at a particular period of pregnancy might cause physical change in the embryo.

Long before breeders had any knowledge of genetics, they practiced one of its most important principles—selective breeding. Experience quickly showed that "like begets like," and by breeding like with like and discarding unlike offspring, the various individual breeds were developed to the point where variations were relatively few. Selective breeding is based on the idea of maintaining the quality of a breed at the highest possible level, while improving whatever defects are prevalent. It requires that only the top dogs in a litter be kept for later breeding, and that inferior specimens be ruthlessly eliminated.

In planning any breeding program, the first requisite is a definite goal—that is, to have clearly in mind a definite picture of the type of dog you wish eventually to produce. To attempt to breed perfection is to approach the problem unrealistically. But if you don't breed for improvement, it is preferable that you not breed at all.

As a first step, you should select a bitch that exemplifies as many of the desired characteristics as possible and mate her with a dog that also has as many of the desired characteristics as possible. If you start with mediocre pets, you will produce mediocre pet puppies. If you decide to start with more than one bitch, all should closely approach the type you desire, since you will

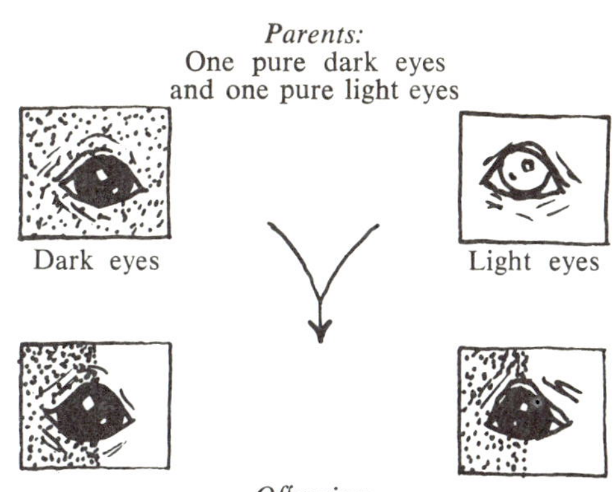

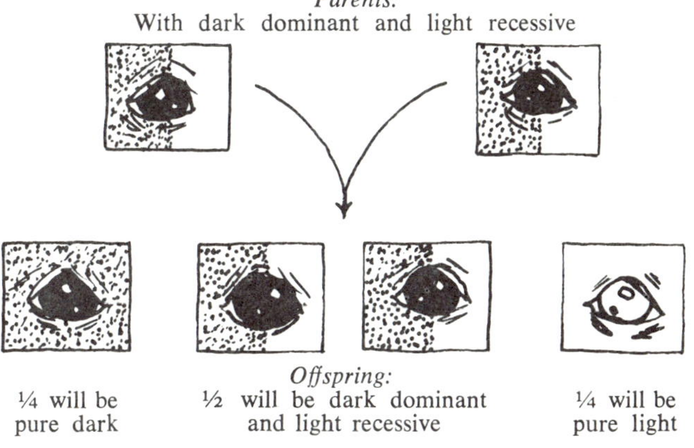

The above is a schematic representation of the Mendelian law as it applies to the inheritance of eye color. The law applies in the same way to the inheritance of other physical characteristics.

then stand a better chance of producing uniformly good puppies from all. Breeders often start with a single bitch and keep the best bitches in every succeeding generation.

Experienced breeders look for "prepotency" in breeding stock —that is, the ability of a dog or bitch to transmit traits to most or all of its offspring. While the term is usually used to describe the transmission of good qualities, a dog may also be prepotent in transmitting faults. To be prepotent in a practical sense, a dog must possess many characteristics controlled by dominant genes. If desired characteristics are recessive, they will be apparent in the offspring only if carried by both sire and dam. Prepotent dogs and bitches usually come from a line of prepotent ancestors, but the mere fact that a dog has exceptional ancestors will not necessarily mean that he himself will produce exceptional offspring.

A single dog may sire a tremendous number of puppies, whereas a bitch can produce only a comparatively few litters during her lifetime. Thus, a sire's influence may be very widespread as compared to that of a bitch. But in evaluating a particular litter, it must be remembered that the bitch has had as much influence as has had the dog.

Inbreeding, line-breeding, outcrossing, or a combination of the three are the methods commonly used in selective breeding.

Inbreeding is the mating together of closely related animals, such as father-daughter, mother-son, or brother-sister. Although some breeders insist such breeding will lead to the production of defective individuals, it is through rigid inbreeding that all breeds of dogs have been established. Controlled tests have shown that any harmful effects appear within the first five or ten generations, and that if rigid selection is exercised from the beginning, a vigorous inbred strain will be built up.

Line-breeding is also the mating together of individuals related by family lines. However, matings are made not so much on the basis of the dog's and bitch's relationship to each other, but, instead, on the basis of their relationship to a highly admired ancestor, with a view to perpetuating his qualities. Line-breeding constitutes a long-range program and cannot be accomplished in a single generation.

Outcrossing is the breeding together of two dogs that are unrelated in family lines. Actually, since breeds have been developed through the mating of close relatives, all dogs within any given breed are related to some extent. There are few breedings that are true outcrosses, but if there is no common ancestor within five generations, a mating is usually considered an outcross.

Experienced breeders sometimes outcross for one generation in order to eliminate a particular fault, then go back to inbreeding or line-breeding. Neither the good effects nor the bad effects of outcrossing can be truly evaluated in a single mating, for undesirable recessive traits may be introduced into a strain, yet not show up for several generations. Outcrossing is better left to experienced breeders, for continual outcrossing results in a wide variation in type and great uncertainty as to the results that may be expected.

Two serious defects that are believed heritable—subluxation and orchidism—should be zealously guarded against, and afflicted dogs and their offspring should be eliminated from breeding programs. Subluxation is a condition of the hip joint where the bone of the socket is eroded and the head of the thigh bone is also worn away, causing lameness which becomes progressively more serious until the dog is unable to walk. Orchidism is the failure of one or both testicles to develop and descend properly. When one testicle is involved, the term "monorchid" is used. When both are involved, "cryptorchid" is used. A cryptorchid is almost always sterile, whereas a monorchid is usually fertile. There is evidence that orchidism "runs in families" and that a monorchid transmits the tendency through bitch and male puppies alike.

Through the years, many misconceptions concerning heredity have been perpetuated. Perhaps the one most widely perpetuated is the idea evolved hundreds of years ago that somehow characteristics were passed on through the mixing of the blood of the parents. We still use terminology evolved from that theory when we speak of bloodlines, or describe individuals as full-blooded, despite the fact that the theory was disproved more than a century ago.

Also inaccurate and misleading is any statement that a definite fraction or proportion of an animal's inherited characteristics can be positively attributed to a particular ancestor. Individuals lacking knowledge of genetics sometimes declare that an individual receives half his inherited characteristics from each parent, a quarter from each grandparent, an eighth from each great-grandparent, etc. Thousands of volumes of scientific findings have been published, but no simple way has been found to determine positively which characteristics have been inherited from which ancestors, for the science of heredity is infinitely complex.

Any breeder interested in starting a serious breeding program should study several of the excellent books on canine genetics that are currently available.

Whelping box. Detail at right shows proper side-wall construction which helps keep small puppies confined and provides sheltered nook which to prevent crushing or smothering.

Breeding and Whelping

The breeding life of a bitch begins when she comes into season the first time at the age of about one to two years (depending on what breed she is). Thereafter, she will come in season at roughly six-month intervals, but this, too, is subject to variation. Her maximum fertility builds up from puberty to full maturity and then declines until a state of total sterility is reached in old age. Just when this occurs is hard to determine, for the fact that an older bitch shows signs of being in season doesn't necessarily mean she is still capable of reproducing.

The length of the season varies from eighteen to twenty-one days. The first indication is a pronounced swelling of the vulva with coincidental bleeding (called "showing color") for about the first seven to nine days. The discharge gradually turns to a creamy color, and it is during this phase (estrus), from about the tenth to the fifteenth days, that the bitch is ovulating and is receptive to the male. The ripe, unfertilized ova survive for about seventy-two hours. If fertilization doesn't occur, the ova die and are discharged the next time the bitch comes in season. If fertilization does take place, each ovum attaches itself to the walls of the uterus, a membrane forms to seal it off, and a foetus develops from it.

Following the estrus phase, the bitch is still in season until about the twenty-first day and will continue to be attractive to males, although she will usually fight them off as she did the first few days. Nevertheless, to avoid accidental mating, the bitch must be confined for the entire period. Virtual imprisonment is necessary, for male dogs display uncanny abilities in their efforts to reach a bitch in season.

The odor that attracts the males is present in the bitch's urine, so it is advisable to take her a good distance from the house before permitting her to relieve herself. To eliminate problems completely, your veterinarian can prescribe a preparation that will disguise the odor but will not interfere with breeding when the time is right. Many fanciers use such preparations when exhibiting a bitch and find that nearby males show no interest whatsoever. But it is not advisable to permit a bitch to run loose when she has been given a product of this type, for during estrus she will seek the company of male dogs and an accidental mating may occur.

A potential brood bitch, regardless of breed, should have good bone, ample breadth and depth of ribbing, and adequate room in the pelvic region. Unless a bitch is physically mature—well beyond the puppy stage when she has her first season—breeding should be delayed until her second or a later season. Furthermore, even though it is possible for a bitch to conceive twice a year, she should not be bred oftener than once a year. A bitch that is bred too often will age prematurely and her puppies are likely to lack vigor.

Two or three months before a bitch is to be mated, her physical condition should be considered carefully. If she is too thin, provide a rich, balanced diet plus the regular exercise needed to develop strong, supple muscles. Daily exercise on the lead is as necessary for the too-thin bitch as for the too fat one, although the latter will need more exercise and at a brisker pace, as well as a reduction of food, if she is to be brought to optimum condition. A prospective brood bitch must have had permanent distemper shots as well as rabies vaccination. And a month before her season is due, a veterinarian should examine a stool specimen for worms. If there is evidence of infestation, the bitch should be wormed.

A dog may be used at stud from the time he reaches physical maturity, well on into old age. The first time your bitch is bred, it is well to use a stud that has already proven his ability by having sired other litters. The fact that a neighbor's dog is readily available should not influence your choice, for to produce the best puppies, you must select the stud most suitable from a genetic standpoint.

If the stud you prefer is not going to be available at the time your bitch is to be in season, you may wish to consult your veterinarian concerning medications available for inhibiting the onset of the season. With such preparations, the bitch's season can be delayed indefinitely.

Usually the first service will be successful. However, if it isn't, in most cases an additional service is given free, provided the stud dog is still in the possession of the same owner. If the bitch misses, it may be because her cycle varies widely from normal. Through microscopic examination, a veterinarian can determine exactly when the bitch is entering the estrus phase and thus is likely to conceive.

The owner of the stud should give you a stud-service certificate, providing a four-generation pedigree for the sire and showing the date of mating. The litter registration application is completed only after the puppies are whelped, but it, too, must be signed by the owner of the stud as well as the owner of the bitch. Registration forms may be secured by writing The American Kennel Club.

In normal pregnancy there is usually visible enlargement of the abdomen by the end of the fifth week. By palpation (feeling with the fingers) a veterinarian may be able to distinguish developing puppies as early as three weeks after mating, but it is unwise for a novice to poke and prod, and try to detect the presence of unborn puppies.

The gestation period normally lasts nine weeks, although it may vary from sixty-one to sixty-five days. If it goes beyond sixty-five days from the date of mating, a veterinarian should be consulted.

During the first four or five weeks, the bitch should be permitted her normal amount of activity. As she becomes heavier, she should be walked on the lead, but strenuous running and jumping should be avoided. Her diet should be well balanced (see page 43), and if she should become constipated, small amounts of mineral oil may be added to her food.

A whelping box should be secured about two weeks before the puppies are due, and the bitch should start then to use it as her bed so she will be accustomed to it by the time puppies arrive. Preferably, the box should be square, with each side long enough so that the bitch can stretch out full length and have several inches to spare at either end. The bottom should be padded with an old cotton rug or other material that is easily laundered. Edges of the padding should be tacked to the floor of the box so the puppies will not get caught in it and smother. Once it is obvious labor is about to begin, the padding should be covered with several layers of spread-out newspapers. Then, as papers become soiled, the top layer can be pulled off, leaving the area clean.

Forty-eight to seventy-two hours before the litter is to be whelped, a definite change in the shape of the abdomen will be noted. Instead of looking barrel-shaped, the abdomen will sag pendulously. Breasts usually redden and become enlarged, and milk may be present a day or two before the puppies are whelped. As the time becomes imminent, the bitch will probably scratch and root at her bedding in an effort to make a nest, and will refuse food and ask to be let out every few minutes. But the surest sign is a drop in temperature of two or three degrees about twelve hours before labor begins.

The bitch's abdomen and flanks will contract sharply when labor actually starts, and for a few minutes she will attempt to expel a puppy, then rest for a while and try again. Someone should stay with the bitch the entire time whelping is taking place, and if she appears to be having unusual difficulties, a veterinarian should be called.

Puppies are usually born head first, though some may be born feet first and no difficulty encountered. Each puppy is enclosed in a separate membranous sac that the bitch will remove with her teeth. She will sever the umbilical cord, which will be attached to the soft, spongy afterbirth that is expelled right after the puppy emerges. Usually the bitch eats the afterbirth, so it is necessary to watch and make sure one is expelled for each puppy whelped. If afterbirth is retained, the bitch may develop peritonitis and die.

The dam will lick and nuzzle each newborn puppy until it is warm and dry and ready to nurse. If puppies arrive so close together that she can't take care of them, you can help her by rubbing the puppies dry with a soft cloth. If several have been whelped but the bitch continues to be in labor, all but one should be removed and placed in a small box lined with clean towels and warmed to about seventy degrees. The bitch will be calmer if one puppy is left with her at all times.

Whelping sometimes continues as long as twenty-four hours for a very large litter, but a litter of two or three puppies may be whelped in an hour. When the bitch settles down, curls around the puppies and nuzzles them to her, it usually indicates that all have been whelped.

The bitch should be taken away for a few minutes while you clean the box and arrange clean padding. If her coat is soiled, sponge it clean before she returns to the puppies. Once she is back in the box, offer her a bowl of warm beef broth and a pan of cool water, placing both where she will not have to get up in order to reach them. As soon as she indicates interest in food, give her a generous bowl of chopped meat to which codliver oil and dicalcium phosphate have been added (see page 43).

If inadequate amounts of calcium are provided during the period the puppies are nursing, eclampsia may develop. Symptoms are violent trembling, rapid rise in temperature, and rigidity of muscles. Veterinary assistance must be secured immediately, for death may result in a very short time. Treatment consists of massive doses of calcium gluconate administered intravenously, after which symptoms subside in a miraculously short time.

All puppies are born blind and their eyes open when they are ten to fourteen days old. At first the eyes have a bluish cast and appear weak, and the puppies must be protected from strong light until at least ten days after the eyes open.

To ensure proper emotional development, young dogs should be shielded from loud noises and rough handling. Being lifted by the front legs is painful and may result in permanent injury to the shoulders. So when lifting a puppy, always place one hand under the chest with the forefinger between the front legs, and place the other hand under his bottom.

Sometimes the puppies' nails are so long and sharp that they scratch the bitch's breasts. Since the nails are soft, they can be trimmed with ordinary scissors.

If of a breed that ordinarily has a docked tail, puppies should have their tails shortened when they are three days old. Dewclaws—thumblike appendages appearing on the inside of the legs of some breeds—are removed at the same time. While both are simple procedures, they shouldn't be attempted by amateurs.

In certain breeds it is customary to crop the ears, also. This should be done at about eight weeks of age. Cropping should never be attempted by anyone other than a veterinarian, for it requires use of anesthesia and knowledge of surgical techniques, as well as judgment as to the eventual size of the dog and proportion of ear to be removed so the head will be balanced when the dog is mature.

At about four weeks of age, formula should be provided. The amount fed each day should be increased over a period of two weeks, when the puppies can be weaned completely. The formula should be prepared as described on page 41, warmed to luke-warm, and poured into a shallow pan placed on the floor of the box. After his mouth has been dipped into the mixture a few times, a puppy will usually start to lap formula. All puppies should be allowed to eat from the same pan, but be sure the small ones get their share. If they are pushed aside, feed them separately. Permit the puppies to nurse part of the time, but gradually increase the number of meals of formula. By the time the puppies are five weeks old, the dam should be allowed with them only at night. When they are about six weeks old, they should be weaned completely and fed the puppy diet described on page 41.

Once they are weaned, puppies should be given temporary distemper injections every two weeks until they are old enough for permanent inoculations. At six weeks, stool specimens should be checked for worms, for almost without exception, puppies become infested. Specimens should be checked again at eight weeks, and as often thereafter as your veterinarian recommends.

Sometimes owners decide as a matter of convenience to have a bitch spayed or a male castrated. While this is recommended when a dog has a serious inheritable defect or when abnormalities of reproductive organs develop, in sound, normal purebred dogs, spaying a bitch or castrating a male may prove a definite disadvantage. The operations automatically bar dogs from competing in shows as well as precluding use for breeding. The operations are seldom dangerous, but they should not be performed without good reason.

Hall of Fame

This chapter is presented in an effort to make available to Lhasa Apso breeders and exhibitors an opportunity to study pictures and pedigrees of some of the dogs that have been winning in the show rings during the last ten years. Pictures occasionally appear in magazines but they are not accompanied with the pedigrees, so little or no evaluation can be made of the breeding program that produced that particular dog. It is hoped that this unit will correct that situation, even if only in a limited way.

The information regarding each dog refers to the period of time when he was on the show circuit. In some cases, ownership may have changed, and in two cases the dog is deceased. It is felt, however, that these dogs have made significant contributions and should, therefore, be included in this section. Some of these dogs are still being campaigned and will accumulate many more awards. There are undoubtedly many other specimens worthy of inclusion here, but limitations of space have made this impossible.

The breeder will have an opportunity to study several generations of a particular line, since an effort has been made to show two or three generations of winners. The dogs are listed in alphabetical order to facilitate the search. It should also be noted that many of these winners are closely line-bred and in some cases, even inbred. There are also examples of outcrosses.

The dogs presented here are representatives from almost all parts of the country. The leading breeding lines are also represented.

Ch. America's Sing Song (D); whelped October 16, 1967; red-gold. H. C. and R. H. Cohrs, Owners and Handlers. K. Given, Judge.

			CH. HAMILTON TATSIENLU
		CH. HAMILTON KALON	
			Hamilton Tughar
	Hamilton Toradga		
			CH. HAMILTON TATSIENLU
		CH. HAMILTON DEN-SA	
America's Sandlwood of Pamu			Hamilton Dobra
			Shan Sun
		Lin-Li-Poo	
	Lady Pamu		Hamilton CaFra
			Sin
		Lo-Tsien	
			Hamilton CaFra
			CH. HAMILTON TATSIENLU
		CH. HAMILTON KALON	
			Hamilton Tughar
	Hamilton Toradga		
			CH. HAMILTON TATSIENLU
		CH. HAMILTON DEN-SA	
America's Sherpo			Hamilton Dobra
			Shan Sun
		Lin-Li-Poo	
	Lady Pamu		Hamilton CaFra
			Sin
		Lo-Tsien	
			Hamilton CaFra

Am. and Can. Ch. Arborhill's Rah-Kieh (D); whelped February 4, 1970; golden; Best in Show. Virginia Knocke and Dr. D. J. Miller, Owners. Dorothy Kendall, Handler. Sharon Binkowski, Breeder.

```
                                              Glen Pines Chagpo-Ri
                        CH. KAI SANGS CLOWN OF EVERGLO
                                              Kai Sangs Tzi-Ren of Miradel
            CH. EVERGLO'S SPARK OF GOLD
                                              CH. KAI SANGS CLOWN OF EVERGLO
                        Tibetan Cookie of Everglo
                                              Ruffway's Hun-Nee-Bun
AM. & CAN. CH. ARBORHILL'S RAPSO-DIEH
                                              CH. KYI CHU KALIPH NOR
                        CH. CHERRYSHORES BAH BIEH BOI
                                              CH. CHERRYSHORES MAH DAHM
            CH. ARBORHILL'S LEE-SAH
                                              CH. JIMPA'S KANA RINPOCHE
                        CH. ARBORHILL'S KAROLING KAROLYN
                                              Gser Jo-Mo of La-Sari

                                              CH. HAMILTON ACHOK
                        Licos Khung-La
                                              CH. LICOS NYAPSO LA
            CH. KAHM OF NORBULINGKA
                                              CH. HAMILTON SANDUPA
                        Karma Kasala
                                              AM. & MEX. CH. KARMA SANGPO
CH. ARBORHILL'S LHANA
                                              CH. HAMILTON JIMPA
                        CH. JIMPA'S KANA RINPOCHE
                                              CH. SHAR MING OF BANGALOR
            CH. ARBORHILL'S KAROLING KAROLYN
                                              Joli Grumpa of Glen Pines
                        Gser Jo-Mo of La-Sari
                                              Shenji's Moppsie
```

Ch. Arborhill's Rapso-Dieh (D); whelped June 30, 1968; golden; Best in Show. Sharon and Robert J. Binkowski, Arborhill Kennels, Breeders and Owners. Jerry Edwards, Handler.

```
                                              Las-Sa-Gre's Hijo D'Altiro
                          Glen Pines Chagpo-Ri
                                              CH. MIRADEL'S NIMA
              CH. KAI SANGS CLOWN OF EVERGLO
                                              CH. LAS-SA-GRE'S MANCHADO DORADO
                          Kai Sangs Tzi-Ren of Miradel
                                              Chika Rinpoche
CH. EVERGLO'S SPARK OF GOLD
                                              Glen Pines Chagpo-Ri
                          CH. KAI SANGS CLOWN OF EVERGLO
                                              Kai Sangs Tzi-Ren of Miradel
              Tibetan Cookie of Everglo
                                              CH. MING FU TZU
                          Ruffway's Hun-Nee-Bun
                                              CH. GLENFLO'S GIRJE


                                              American's Sandar of Pamu
                          CH. KYI CHU KALIPH NOR
                                              CH. KARMA AMI CHIRI
              CH. CHERRYSHORES BAH BIEH BOI
                                              CH. CHU-LA'S MIEH T'U
                          CH. CHERRYSHORES MAH DAHM
                                              Green Diamond Decidedly
CH. ARBORHILL'S LEE-SAH
                                              CH. HAMILTON JIMPA
                          CH. JIMPA'S KANA RINPOCHE
                                              CH. SHAR MING OF BANGALOR
              CH. ARBORHILL'S KAROLING KAROLYN
                                              Joli Grumpa of Glen Pines
                          Gser Jo-Mo of La-Sari
                                              Shenji's Moppsie
```

Ch. Bar-Con's The Avenger (D); whelped August 26, 1970; golden; Best in Show. Dorothy J. Kendall, Co-Owner and Handler. Barry and Connie Tompkins, Breeders and Co-Owners. Dr. Robert J. Berndt, Judge.

<pre>
                                              Las-Sa-Gre's Hijo D'Altiro
                           Glen Pine's Chagpo-Ri
                                              CH. MIRADEL'S NIMA
              CH. KAI SANGS CLOWN OF EVERGLO
                                              CH. LAS-SA-GRE'S MANCHADO DORADO
                           Kai Sang Tzi-Ren of Miradel
                                              Chika Rinpoche
CH. EVERGLO'S SPARK OF GOLD
                                              Glen Pine's Chagpo-Ri
                           CH. KAI SANGS CLOWN OF EVERGLO
                                              Kai-Sang Tzi-Ren of Miradel
              Tibetan Cookie of Everglo
                                              CH. MING FU TZU
                           Ruffway's Hun-Nee Bun
                                              CH. GLENFLO'S GIRJE

                                              Karma Tharpa
                           CH. TIBET OF CORNWALLIS
                                              CH. LICOS CHETI-LA
              CH. KEKE'S PETRUCHIO
                                              CH. KARMA KANJUR
                           CH. KYI-CHU SHARA
                                              CH. KYI-CHU KIRA, C. D.
Bar-Con's Madam Eglantyne
                                              CH. RAGGS OF CORNWALLIS
                           CH. MR. KAY OF CORNWALLIS
                                              Rema of Cornwallis
              Keke's Little Ginger
                                              CH. HAMILTON NAMSA
                           CH. KEKE'S T'CHIN T'CHIN
                                              Smedley's Seeou Ying
</pre>

Ch. Berano's Hop-Sun-Tsu (D); whelped January 6, 1968; golden. Bea and Ralph Gutelius, Berano Kennels, Breeders, Owners, and Handlers. A. Rosenberg, Judge.

<pre>
                                                      Stittig's Pao Tzo Cee
                                Stittig's Jumma Deimar
                                                      Stittig's Moka Kara Deimar
          CH. MAIDA MANORS SANMAN
                                                      Dakmar of Champlain View
                                CH. LYNCHAVEN GURLA
                                                      CH. YAY SIH OF SHEBO
CH. MAIDA MANORS SUNSET
                                                      CH. LAS-SA-GRE'S MANCHADO DORADO
                                Valeta's Monga Fu O'Kenmore
                                                      Chika Rinpoche
          Maida Manors Masiene
                                                      Chado of Miradel
                                Nanvirlu's Ling Kyi
                                                      Wee Tschechockling

                                                      CH. AMERICAL'S TORMA LU
                                CH. KARMA NAROPA
                                                      CH. KARMA SANGPO
          Cherryshore's Hah Tsot
                                                      CH. CHU-LA'S MIEH T'U
                                CH. CHERRYSHORES MAH DAHM
                                                      Green Diamond Decidedly
Berano's Hah-Ni-Soo
                                                      Americal's Sandar of Pamu
                                CH. KYI-CHU KALIPH NOR
                                                      CH. KARMA AMI CHIRI
          CH. CHERRYSHORES TING-A-LING
                                                      CH. AMERICAL'S TORMA LU
                                CH. CHERRYSHORES MAH DAHM
                                                      CH. KARMA SANG-PO
</pre>

Ch. Everglo's Spark of Gold (D); whelped May 23, 1963; golden; Best in Show. Dorothy Kendall, Orlane Kennels, Owner. Everglo Kennel, Breeder. C. Hamilton, Judge.

<pre>
                                                            CH. FU LA TIRITO
                                        Las-Sa-Gre's Hijo D'Altiro
                                                            CH. FU LA DIABLITA
                        Glen Pines Chagpo-Ri
                                                            CH. MING TALI II, C. D.
                                        CH. MIRADEL'S NIMA
                                                            Miradel's Fa Li
        CH. KAI SANGS CLOWN OF EVERGLO
                                                            CH. FU LA TIRITO
                                        CH. LAS-SA-GRE'S MANCHADO DORADO
                                                            CH. FU LA DIABLITA
                        Kai Sang Tzi-Ren of Miradel
                                                            CH. HAMILTON SANDUR
                                        Chika Rinpoche
                                                            CH. YAY SIH OF SHEBO

                                                            Las-Sa-Gre's Hijo D'Altiro
                                        Glen Pines Chagpo-Ri
                                                            CH. MIRADEL'S NIMA
                        CH. KAI SANGS CLOWN OF EVERGLO
                                                            CH. LAS-SA-GRE'S MANCHADO DORADO
                                        Kai Sang Tzi-Ren of Miradel
                                                            Chika Rinpoche
        Tibetan Cookie of Everglo
                                                            CH. MING TALI II, C. D.
                                        CH. MING FU TZU
                                                            Miradel Khan Du
                        Ruffway's Hun-Nee-Bun
                                                            Las-Sa-Gre's Hijo D'Altiro
                                        CH. GLENFLO'S GIRJE
                                                            CH. MIRADEL'S NIMA
</pre>

Ch. Geradene's Mon-Po-Chi-Py (D); whelped October 23, 1968; golden. Bea and Ralph Gutelius, Berano Kennels, Owners and Handlers. C. Marck, Judge.

                                          CH. AMERICAL'S LENG KONG

                            CH. LICOS KULU LA

                                            CH. AMERICAL'S RIKA

                CH. LICOS OMORFO LA

                                            Hamilton Sandapu

                            CH. HAMILTON PLUTI

                                          Hamilton Den-Sa

AM. CAN. BER. CH. LICOS SINGI LA

                                          CH. AMERICAL'S LENG KONG

                            CH. LICOS KULU LA

                                          CH. AMERICAL'S RIKA

        Dama's Lu Country Fair

                                          CH. HAMILTON ACHOK

                        Licos Dama La

                                          CH. LICOS NYAPSO LA

                                          American's Sandar of Pamu

                            CH. KYI CHU KALIPH NOR

                                          CH. KARMA AMI CHIRI

            CH. CHERRYSHORES BAH BIEH BOI

                                          CH. CHU-LA'S MIEH T'U

                            CH. CHERRYSHORES MAH DAHM

                                        Green Diamond Decidedly

CH. CHERRYSHORES AH SU MING

                                          CH. AMERICAL'S TORMA LU

                            CH. KARMA NAROPA

                                          CH. KARMA SANGPO

            CH. AVARICK'S SOUTHERN BELLE

                                        CH. HAMILTON SANDUPA

                        Hamilton Kyang Tru

                                          Hamilton Mala

Ch. Glenn's Pines Nanda Devi (B); whelped March 12, 1963; golden. Dr. Robert J. Berndt, Owner and Handler. Mr. and Mrs. Robert B. Chambers, Breeders. M. Riddle, Judge.

<pre>
                                                        Hamilton Yangchen
                                    CH. HAMILTON TATSIENLU
                                                        Hamilton Novo
                 CH. HAMILTON ACHOK
                                                        CH. HAMILTON TATSIENLU
                                    Hamilton Dobra
                                                        Hamilton Tughar
CH. SHANGRI-LA RAJAN OF GLEN PINES
                                                        Hamilton Dakmar
                                    Dakmar of Champlain View
                                                        Hamilton Linga
                 Lynchaven Tangla
                                                        CH. WU TAI
                                    Lynchaven Yay Pitchika
                                                        CH. YAY SIH OF SHEBO

                                                        CH. HAMILTON TATSIENLU
                                    CH. HAMILTON ACHOK
                                                        Hamilton Dobra
                 Shangri-La-Dari Achok
                                                        Tibetan Om-Mani Padme-Hum
                                    Tara Tso of Shangri-La
                                                        Lynchaven Tangla
Tongsa of Glenn's Pines
                                                        CH. WU TAI
                                    CH. MING TALI II, C. D.
                                                        CH. MING KYI
                 Miradel's Ama Dablam
                                                        Frazier's Jon of Lost Horizons
                                    Miradel's Fa Li
                                                        Diminutive Delight
</pre>

Ch. Glenn Pine's Ringka (B); whelped October 28, 1962; golden. Dr. Robert J. Berndt, Owner and Handler. Florence Bagley, Breeder. E. McQwon, Judge.

<pre>
                                                      Hamilton Yangchen
                                    CH. HAMILTON TATSIENLU
                                                      Hamilton Novo
                 CH. HAMILTON ACHOK
                                                      CH. HAMILTON TATSIENLU
                                    Hamilton Dobra
                                                      Hamilton Tughar
CH. SHANGRI-LA RAJAN OF GLEN PINES
                                                      Hamilton Dakmar
                                    Dakmar of Champlain View
                                                      Hamilton Linga
                 Lynchaven Tangla
                                                      CH. WU TAI
                                    Lynchaven Yay Pitchika
                                                      CH. YAY SIH OF SHEBO

                                                      Hamilton Dakmar
                                    CH. WU TAI
                                                      CH. MING LU
                 CH. MING TALI II, C. D.
                                                      Pedro
                                    CH. MING KYI
                                                      CH. MING LU
CH. MIRADEL'S NIMA
                                                      Lamasery Bub
                                    Frazer's Jon of Lost Horizons
                                                      Prancing Paltch
                 Miradel's Fa Li
                                                      Lamasery Bub
                                    Diminutive Delight
                                                      Shantra of Tufan
</pre>

Ch. Jerec's Char-La Wa (B); Whelped September 4, 1970; golden; Group I. Mrs. J. R. Ditton, Jerec Kennels, Owner. Marjorie Lewis, Handler. Mrs. M. Heald, Judge.

			CH. LICOS OMORFO LA
		Chen Makalu Nor of Dzungar	
			Kyi-Chu Kara Nor
	Chen Nyun Ti		
			CH. LICOS CHULUNG LA
		Licos Gia La	
			CH. HAMILTON PLUTI
CH. SHARBO ZIJUH SPANGGUR			
			CH. KARMA KUSHOG
		CH. ZIJUH TSAM	
			CH. HAMILTON SHIM TRU
	Zijuh Jinda		
			CH. KARMA LOBSANG
		Donna Cardella's Tsng	
			Karma Dakini
			Karma Taktser
		Karma Heki	
			Hamilton Amdo
	Everglo Albert		
			Cubbi Kyeri of Everglo
		Fern's Flame of Tibet	
			Kambu of Everglo
Mac-Jay Jill of Golden Rule's			
			CH. HAMILTON ACHOK
		CH. LICOS CHULUNG LA	
			CH. LICOS NYAPSO LA
	Golden Rule's Mel-O-Ne O'Everglo		
			CH. LICOS OMORFO LA
		Everglo Buttercup	
			Kyima of Everglo

Am. and Can. Ch. Keepsake (D); whelped October 26, 1961; silver. Dr. Robert J. Berndt, Owner and Handler. M. Crozier and J. Bellany, Breeders. I. Schoenberg, Judge.


```
                                          Hamilton Yangchen
                         CH. HAMILTON TATSIENLU
                                          Hamilton Novo
            CH. HAMILTON ACHOK
                                          CH. HAMILTON TATSIENLU
                         Hamilton Dobra
                                          Hamilton Tughar
CAN. CH. SHANGRI-LA MANA ACHOK
                                          Hamilton Dakmar
                         Dakmar of Champlain View
                                          Hamilton Linga
            Lynchaven Tangla
                                          CH. WU TAI
                         Lynchaven Ya Pitchika
                                          CH. YAY SIH OF SHEBO


                                          CH. HAMILTON TATSIENLU
                         CH. HAMILTON ACHOK
                                          Hamilton Dobra
            Shangri-La Mr. Jigme H. Achok
                                          CH. HAMILTON KALON
                         CH. AMERICAL'S TORMA TSING
                                          CH. HAMILTON TORMA
CAN. CH. SHANGRI-LA DARSHI
                                          Hamilton Nyang
                         Hamilton Pata
                                          Hamilton Sonak
            Lynchaven Cum-Ba-Mia-Yid
                                          Dakmar of Champlain View
                         CH. LYNCHAVEN GURLA
                                          CH. YAY SIH OF SHEBO
```

Am. and Ber. Ch. Kinderland's Tonka (B); whelped August 28, 1968; red-gold; Best in Show. Mr. and Mrs. Norman L. Herbel, Tabu Kennels, Owners. Ellen Lonigro, Breeder.

			CH. HAMILTON SANDUPA
		Karma Yon-Ten	
			Karma Zurwang
	Karma Tharpa		
			America's Sandar of Pamu
		Karma Kam-Bu	
			Hamilton Khib-Tru
CH. TIBET OF CORNWALLIS			
			CH. HAMILTON ACHOK
		CH. LICOS CHAPLIA LA	
			CH. LICOS KARO LA
	CH. LICOS CHETI LA		
			CH. AMERICAL'S LENG KONG
		CH. LICOS NYAPSO LA	
			CH. AMERICAL'S RIKA
			CH. HAMILTON ACHOK
		Licos Khurg La	
			CH. LICOS NYAPSO LA
	CH. KHAM OF NORBULINGKA		
			CH. HAMILTON SANDUPA
		Karma Kosala	
			CH. KARMA SANG-PO
CH. KINDERLAND'S SANG-PO			
			CH. LAS-SA-GRE'S MANCHADO DORADO
		Dzin-Po Rinpoche	
			Chika Rinpoche
	Ch'Ha-Ya-Chi		
			Kepa Rinpoche
		Run-Si Rinpoche	
			CH. TASHI RINPOCHE

Ch. Kyi-Chu Shara (B); whelped July 6, 1964; golden; Best in Show. Keke Blumberg, Potala Kennels, Owner. Terry Smith, Breeder. Connie Blumberg, Handler.


```
                                                      Hamilton Yang Chen
                                    CH. HAMILTON TATSIENLU
                                                      Hamilton Novo
                  Hamilton Maroh
                                                      Hamilton Urga
                                    Hamilton Tigu
                                                      Hamilton Dobra
CH. KARMA KANJUR
                                                      CH. HAMILTON TATSIENLU
                                    CH. HAMILTON KUNG
                                                      Hamilton Dobra
                  CH. KARMA GYAPSO
                                                      Hamilton Maroh
                                    CH. HAMILTON KARMA
                                                      Hamilton Docheno

                                                      CH. HAMILTON TATSIENLU
                                    CH. HAMILTON KALON
                                                      Hamilton Tughar
                  CH. HAMILTON JIMPA
                                                      CH. HAMILTON TATSIENLU
                                    CH. HAMILTON SAMADA
                                                      Hamilton Lachen
CH. KYI-CHU KIRA, C. D.
                                                      Rican of Kelea
                                    CH. COLARLIE'S SHAN BANGALOR
                                                      Au Wu Ting Ling
                  CH. COLARLIE'S MISS SHANDHA
                                                      CH. MING TALI II, C. D.
                  Miradel's Ming Fu Chia, C. D.
                                                      CH. FU LA SIMPATICA
```

Ch. Maida Manors Sunset (D);
whelped January 3, 1961; golden;
Group I. Bea and Ralph Gutelius,
Berano Kennels, Owners. N.
Radcliff, Handler. Dr. W. Mitten,
Judge.

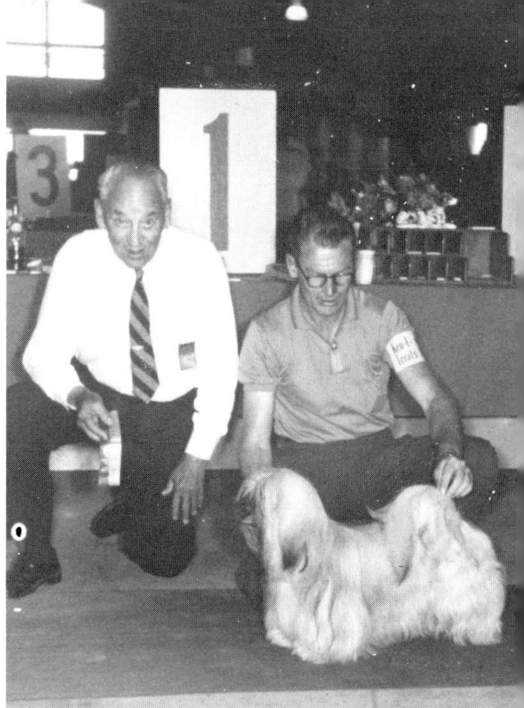


```
                                                      Po Yao Cheng of Masque
                                   Stittig's Pao Tzo Cee
                                                      Si-San of Masque
                  Stittig's Jumma Deimar
                                                      CH. HAMILTON PEKING
                                   Stittig's Moka Kara Deimar
                                                      Hamilton Durga
CH. MAIDA MANORS SAN MAN
                                                      Hamilton Dakmar
                                   Dakmar of Champlain View
                                                      Hamilton Linga
                  CH. LYNCHAVEN GURLA
                                                      Shebo Schunde of Hungjao
                                   CH. YAY SIH OF SHEBO
                                                      Yi of Taisman


                                                      CH. FU LA TIRITO
                                   CH. LAS-SA-GRE'S MANCHADO DORADO
                                                      CH. FU LA DIABLITA
                  Valeta's Monga Fu O'Kenmore
                                                      Hamilton Sandur
                                   Chika Rinpoche
                                                      CH. YAY SIH OF SHEBO
Maida Manors Masiene
                                                      CH. LAS-SA-GRE'S MANCHADO DORADO
                                   Chado of Miradel
                                                      Miradel's Khan Du
                  Nanvirlu's Ling Kyi
                                                      CH. MING TALI II, C. D.
                                   Wee Tschechockling
                                                      Miradel's Chomolung
```

Ch. Maraja's Tsering Momo (D); whelped July 4, 1963; parti-golden-white; Best in Show. Jane and Raymond Bunse, Maraja Kennels, Breeders and Owners.


```
                                                   CH. LAS-SA-GRE'S MANCHADO DORADO
                              Taylor's Chado of Miradel
                                                   Miradel's Khan Dee, C. D.
            CH. COUNTRY FAIR'S KUSHIKHAN
                                                   CH. LAS-SA-GRE'S MANCHADO DORADO
                              Country Fair's Daisy Mae
                                                   Miradel's Chomo Lungma
CH. RUFFWAY TSONG KAPA
                                                   CH. LAS-SA-GRE'S MANCHADO DORADO
                              CH. TAYLOR'S MING OF MIRADEL
                                                   Miradel's Khan Dee, C. D.
            CH. MIRADEL'S DINAH MIGHT
                                                   CH. LAS-SA-GRE'S MANCHADO DORADO
                              Kali of Miradel
                                                   Karma Rinpoche

                                                   Hamilton Dakmar
                              CH. WU TAI
                                                   CH. MING LU
            CH. MING TALI II, C. D.
                                                   Pedro
                              CH. MING KYI
                                                   CH. MING LU
Miradel's Yung Chen of Ruffway
                                                   CH. WU TAI
                              CH. MING TALI II, C. D.
                                                   CH. MING KYI
            CH. DINKES MIRADEL CHEN YANG, C. D.
                                                   CH. LAS-SA-GRE'S MANCHADO DORADO
                              Torlona's Mancho Mink Diki
                                                   Miradel's Chomo Lungma
```

Ch. Martin's Kiwi Puff (D); whelped June 1, 1967; golden; Group I. Rena Martin, Martin's Kennels, Breeder, Owner, and Handler.

<pre>
                                        Hamilton Maroh
                         CH. HAMILTON CHANG-TANG
                                        CH. HAMILTON SAMADA
            America's Sandar of Pamu
                                        Lin-Li-Poo
                         Lady Pamu
                                        Lo-Tsien
CH. KYI-CHU KALIPH NOR
                                        CH. HAMILTON SANDUPA
                         Hamilton Shi-Pon
                                        CH. HAMILTON DEN-SA
            CH. KARMA AMI CHIRI
                                        Hamilton Maroh
                         CH. HAMILTON KARMA
                                        Hamilton Docheno

                                        CH. HAMILTON CHANG-TANG
                         America's Sandar of Pamu
                                        Lady Pamu
            CH. KARMA DMAR-PO
                                        CH. HAMILTON KUNG
                         MEX. & AM. CH. KARMA SANGPO
                                        CH. HAMILTON KARMA
CH. KARMA CRICKET PUFF
                                        CH. HAMILTON TATSIENLU
                         CH. HAMILTON SANDUPA
                                        Hamilton Docheno
            Hamilton Gyo-Tru
                                        CH. HAMILTON KALON
                         Hamilton Mala
                                        Hamilton Tigu
</pre>

Ch. Martin's Kola Puff (D); whelped September 8, 1968; black; Group I. Rena Martin, Martin's Kennels, Breeder, Owner, and Handler.

```
                                                    CH. HAMILTON TATSIENLU
                                CH. HAMILTON KALON
                                                    Hamilton Tughar
              CH. HAMILTON JIMPA
                                                    CH. HAMILTON TATSIENLU
                                CH. HAMILTON SAMADA
                                                    Hamilton Lachen
CH. ZIJUH TASHI
                                                    CH. HAMILTON KUNG
                                CH. KARMA LOBSANG
                                                    CH. HAMILTON KARMA
                    Donna Cardella's Tsng
                                                    CH. HAMILTON SANDUPA
                                Karma Dakini
                                                    MEX. & AM. CH. KARMA SANGPO


                                                    CH. HAMILTON CHANG-TANG
                                America's Sandar of Pamu
                                                    Lady Pamu
              CH. KARMA DMAR-PO
                                                    CH. HAMILTON KUNG
                                MEX. & AM. CH. KARMA SANGPO
                                                    CH. HAMILTON KARMA
CH. KARMA CRICKET PUFF
                                                    CH. HAMILTON TATSIENLU
                                CH. HAMILTON SANDUPA
                                                    Hamilton Docheno
                    Hamilton Gyo-Tru
                                                    CH. HAMILTON KALON
                                Hamilton Mala
                                                    Hamilton Tigu
```

Ch. Maytime Kublai Khan (D);
whelped May 31, 1967; silver. Jack
and Dorothy Slade, Maytime
Kennels, Breeders and Owners.
Peggy Hogg, Handler.

```
                                                              CH. HAMILTON TATSIENLU
                                        CH. HAMILTON ACHOK
                                                              Hamilton Dobra
                         CAN. CH. SHANGRI-LA MANA ACHOK
                                                              Dakmar of Champlain View
                                        Lynchaven Tangle
                                                              Lynchaven Yay Pitchika
          AM. & CAN. CH. KEEPSAKE
                                                              CH. HAMILTON ACHOK
                                        Shangri-La Mr. Jigme H. Achok
                                                              CH. AMERICAL'S TORMA TSING
                         CAN. CH. SHANGRI-LA DARSHI
                                                              Hamilton Pata
                                        Lynchaven Cum-Ba-Mia-Yid
                                                              CH. LYNCHAVEN GURLA

                                                              CH. HAMILTON KALON
                                        CH. HAMILTON JIMPA
                                                              CH. HAMILTON SAMADO
                         CH. QUETZAL FEYLA OF KYI CHU
                                                              CH. COLARLIE'S SHAN BANGALOR
                                        CH. COLARLIE'S MISS SHANDA
                                                              Miradel's Ming Fu Chai, C. D.
          CH. MAYTIME WINNIE-THE-POOH
                                                              CH. HAMILTON ACHOK
                                        CAN. CH. SHANGRI-LA MANA ACHOK
                                                              Lynchaven Tangla
                         AM. & CAN. CH. CAPRICE'S TSAN TE
                                                              Shangri-La Den-nis
                                        Shangri-La Fan Tan
                                                              Tara Tsoo of Shangri-La
```

147

Ch. Maytime Princess O'Berano (B); whelped February 2, 1966; parti-golden-silver-white. Dr. Robert J. Berndt, Owner and Handler. Berano Kennels, Breeder. Mrs. C. Cass, Judge.

			CH. HAMILTON ACHOK
		CAN. CH. SHANGRI-LA MANA ACHOK	
			Lynchaven Tangla
	AM. & CAN. CH. KEEPSAKE		
			Shangri-La Mr. Jigme H. Achok
		CAN. CH. SHANGRI-LA DARSHI	
			Lynchaven Cum-Ba-Mia-Yid
CH. MORGANTOWN'S BOB-O-LOUIE			
			CH. HAMILTON ACHOK
		CAN. CH. SHANGRI-LA MANA ACHOK	
			Lynchaven Tangla
	AM. & CAN. CH. CAPRICE'S TSAN TE		
			Shangri-La Den-nis
		Shangri-La Fan Tan	
			Tara Tsoo of Shangri-La
			Stittig's Jumma Deimar
		CH. MAIDA MANOR'S SANMAN	
			CH. LYNCHAVEN GURLA
	CH. BERANO'S TANG WOO		
			CH. MAIDA MANOR'S SANMAN
		CH. MAIDA MANOR'S SUNRISE	
			Maida Manor's Masiene
CH. BERANO'S LITTLE PRINCESS			
			CH. COUNTRY FAIR'S KUSNIKHAN
		CH. RUFFWAY TSONG KAPA	
			CH. MIRADEL'S DINAH MIGHT
	Taenia-De of Su-Ling		
			Colarlie's Mikado
		Su-Ling of Lic-King	
			Tui Ming Kicka Po Dee Jo Bar

Ch. Morgantown's Bob-O-Louie
(D); whelped November 28, 1963;
silver. Peggy Hogg, Breeder,
Owner, and Handler.

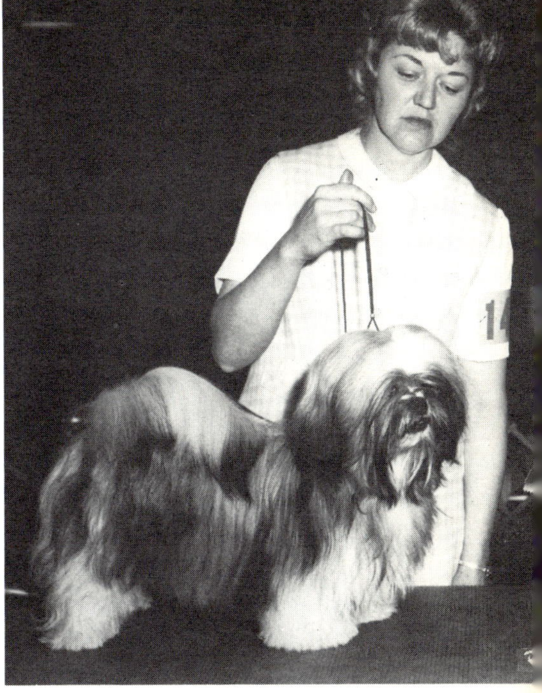

<pre>
                                                    CH. HAMILTON TATSIENLU
                                CH. HAMILTON ACHOK
                                                    Hamilton Dobra
                CAN. CH. SHANGRI-LA MANA ACHOK
                                                    Dakmar of Champlain View
                                Lynchaven Tangla
                                                    Lynchaven Yay Pitchka
        AM. & CAN. CH. KEEPSAKE
                                                    CH. HAMILTON ACHOK
                                Shangri-La Mr. Jigme H. Achok
                                                    CH. AMERICAL'S TORMA TSING
                CAN. CH. SHANGRI-LA DARSHI
                                                    Hamilton Pata
                                Lynchaven Cum-Ba Mai-Yid
                                                    CH. LYNCHAVEN GURLA

                                                    CH. HAMILTON TATSIENLU
                                CH. HAMILTON ACHOK
                                                    Hamilton Dobra
                CAN. CH. SHANGRI-LA ACHOK
                                                    Dakmar of Champlain View
                                Lynchaven Tangla
                                                    Lynchaven Yay Pitchika
        AM. & CAN. CH. CAPRICE'S TSAN TE
                                                    CH. TENZING OF LOST HORIZONS
                                Shangri-La Den-nis
                                                    Shangri-La Tata Tina Mia
                Shangri-La Fan Tan
                                                    Tibetan Om-Mani Padme-Hum
                                Tara Tsoo of Shangri-La
                                                    Lynchaven Tangla
</pre>

Ch. Orlane's Be-Sparky of Al-Mar (D); whelped June 11, 1970; red-gold; Best in Show.
Marjorie Lewis, Al-Mar Kennels, Owner and Handler. Dorothy Kendall, Breeder.
L. E. Piper, Judge.

```
                                                   Glen Pines Chagpo-Ri
                                 CH. KAI SANGS CLOWN OF EVERGLO
                                                   Kai Sangs Tzi-Ren of Miradel
              CH. EVERGLO'S SPARK OF GOLD
                                                   CH. KAI SANGS CLOWN OF EVERGLO
                                 Tibetan Cookie of Everglo
                                                   Ruffway's Hun-Nee-Bun
CH. ORLANE'S DIEH BIEH
                                                   CH. KARMA KUSHOG
                                 CH. KARMA FROSTY KNIGHT O EVERGLO
                                                   CH. HAMILTON SHA-TRU
              CH. ORLANE'S CHITRA OF RUFFWAY
                                                   Cubbi Kyeri of Everglo
                                 Ruffway Khambu
                                                   Stittig's Moka-Kara Deimar


                                                   Glen Pines Chagpo-Ri
                                 CH. KAI SANGS CLOWN OF EVERGLO
                                                   Kai Sangs Tzi-Ren of Miradel
              CH. EVERGLO'S SPARK OF GOLD
                                                   CH. KAI SANGS CLOWN OF EVERGLO
                                 Tibetan Cookie of Everglo
                                                   Ruffway's Hun-Nee-Bun
Orlane's Holly Berry
                                                   Glen Pines Chagpo-Ri
                                 CH. KAI SANGS CLOWN OF EVERGLO
                                                   Kai Sangs Tzi-Ren of Miradel
              CH. KAI SANGS FLAME OF EVERGLO
                                                   CH. HAMILTON SANDUPA
                                 Hamilton Norden
                                                   CH. HAMILTON DEN-SA
```

Ch. Orlane's Dulmo (D); whelped June 5, 1967; grizzle. Larry W. Smith, Yat-Sen Kennels, Owner. Dorothy Kendall, Breeder.

```
                                          Las-Sa-Gre's Hijo D'Altiro
                          Glen Pines Chagpo-Ri
                                          CH. MIRADEL'S NIMA
              CH. KAI SANGS CLOWN OF EVERGLO
                                          CH. LAS-SA-GRE'S MANCHADO DORADO
                          Kai Sangs Tzi-Ren of Miradel
                                          Chika Rinpoche
CH. EVERGLO'S SPARK OF GOLD
                                          Glen Pines Chagpo-Ri
                          CH. KAI SANGS CLOWN OF EVERGLO
                                          Kai Sangs Tzi-Ren of Miradel
              Tibetan Cookie of Everglo
                                          CH. MIRADEL'S MING FU TZU
                          Ruffway's Hun-Nee-Bun
                                          CH. GLENFLO'S GIRJE


                                          Hamilton Shi-Pon
                          CH. KARMA KUSHOG
                                          CH. HAMILTON KARMA
              CH. KARMA FROSTY KNIGHT OF EVERGLO
                                          CH. HAMILTON SANDUPA
                          CH. HAMILTON SHA-TRU
                                          Hamilton Gharpon
CH. ORLANE'S CHITRA OF RUFFWAY
                                          CH. LICOS CHULUNG LA
                          Cubbi Kyeri of Everglo
                                          Hamilton Norden
              Ruffway Khambu
                                          CH. HAMILTON PEKING
                          Stittig's Moka-Kara Deimar
                                          Hamilton Durga
```

Am. and Can. Ch. Orlane's Good As Gold (B); whelped May 8, 1965; golden; Best in Show. Dorothy Kendall, Orlane Kennels, Breeder and Owner. Jerry Edwards, Handler.

<pre>
                                                                  CH. HAMILTON TATSIENLU
                                        CH. HAMILTON KALON
                                                                  CH. HAMILTON TUGHAR
                   CH. HAMILTON JIMPA
                                                                  CH. HAMILTON TATSIENLU
                                        CH. HAMILTON SAMADA
                                                                  Hamilton Lachen
CH. QUETZAL FEYLA OF KYI-CHU
                                                                  Rican of Kelea
                                        CH. COLARLIE'S SHAN BANGALOR
                                                                  Ai Wu Ting Ling
                   CH. COLARLIE'S MISS SHANDHA
                                                                  CH. MING TALI II, C. D.
                   Miradel's Ming Fu Chia, C. D.
                                                                  CH. FU LA SIMPATICA

                                                                  Las-Sa-Gre's Hijo D'Altiro
                   Glen Pine's Chagpo-Ri
                                                                  CH. MIRADEL'S NIMA
                   CH. KAI SANGS CLOWN OF EVERGLO
                                                                  CH. LAS-SA-GRE'S MANCHADO DORADO
                   Kai Sang Tzi-Ren of Miradel
                                                                  Chika Rinpoche
CH. KAI SANGS FLAME OF EVERGLO
                                                                  CH. HAMILTON TATSIENLU
                                        CH. HAMILTON SANDUPA
                                                                  Hamilton Docheno
                   Hamilton Norden
                                                                  CH. HAMILTON TATSIENLU
                                        CH. HAMILTON DEN-SA
                                                                  Hamilton Dobra
</pre>

Ch. Orlane's Tiger Burning Bright (D); whelped April 29, 1968; golden. Dr. Robert J. Berndt, Owner and Handler. Dorothy Kendall, Breeder.

```
                                                      Glen Pines Chagpo-Ri
                                  CH. KAI SANGS CLOWN OF EVERGLO
                                                      Kai Sangs Tzi-Ren of Miradel
             CH. EVERGLO'S SPARK OF GOLD
                                                      CH. KAI SANGS CLOWN OF EVERGLO
                         Tibetan Cookie of Everglo
                                                      Ruffway's Hun-Nee-Bun
CH. ORLANE'S DULMO
                                                      CH. KARMA KUSHOG
                                  CH. KARMA FROSTY KNIGHT O EVERGLO
                                                      CH. HAMILTON SHA-TRU
                 CH. ORLANE'S CHITRA OF RUFFWAY
                                                      Cubbi Kyeri of Everglo
                         Ruffway Khambu
                                                      Stittig's Moka-Kara Deimar


                                                      Glen Pines Chagpo-Ri
                                  CH. KAI SANGS CLOWN OF EVERGLO
                                                      Kai Sangs Tzi-Ren of Miradel
             CH. EVERGLO'S SPARK OF GOLD
                                                      CH. KAI SANGS CLOWN OF EVERGLO
                         Tibetan Cookie of Everglo
                                                      Ruffway's Hun-Nee-Bun
Orlane's Ransi of Dorken
                                                      CH. LICOS CHULUNG LA
                         Cubbi Kyeri of Everglo
                                                      Hamilton Norden
             Ruffway Khambu
                                                      CH. HAMILTON PEKING
                         Stittig's Moka-Kara Deimar
                                                      Hamilton Durga
```

Ch. Potala Keke's Tomba Tu (D); whelped September 28, 1970; golden; Group I. Keke Blumberg, Potala Kennels, Breeder and Owner. Carolyn Herbel, Handler. Mrs. C. Cass, Judge.

<pre>
                                        Hamilton Shi-Pon
                           CH. KARMA KUSHOG
                                        CH. HAMILTON KARMA
               CH. KARMA FROSTY KNIGHT O EVERGLO
                                        CH. HAMILTON SANDUPA
                           CH. HAMILTON SHA-TRU
                                        Hamilton Gharpon
CH. EVERGLO ZIJUH TOMBA
                                        CH. LICOS CHULUNG LA
                           Cubbi Kyeri of Everglo
                                        Hamilton Norden
               Kambu of Everglo
                                        Hamilton Yi-Tru
                           CH. KYIMA OF EVERGLO
                                        Stittig's Moka Kara Deimar

                                        CH. HAMILTON KALON
                           Hamilton Toradga
                                        CH. HAMILTON DEN-SA
               CH. ZIJUH SENG-TRU
                                        CH. HAMILTON SANDUPA
                           CH. HAMILTON SHIM-TRU
                                        Hamilton Saung
AM. & CAN. CH. POTALA KEKE'S YUM YUM
                                        Karma Tharpa
                           CH. TIBET OF CORNWALLIS
                                        CH. LICOS CHETI-LA
               CH. KEKE'S BAMBOO
                                        CH. KHAM OF NORBULINGKA
                           CH. KEKE'S T'CHIN TING T'CHIN
                                        CH. KEKE'S T'CHIN T'CHIN
</pre>

Ch. Potala Kinderland's Goliath (D); whelped February 15, 1970; golden; Group I.
Mrs. J. R. Ditton, Jerec Kennels, Owner. Ellen Lonigro, Breeder. Dee Shepherd,
Handler. A. Stamm, Judge.

<pre>
                                                Glen Pine's Chagpo-Ri
                              CH. KAI SANGS CLOWN OF EVERGLO
                                                Kai Sang Tzi-Ren of Miradel
              CH. EVERGLO'S SPARK OF GOLD
                                                CH. KAI SANGS CLOWN OF EVERGLO
                              Tibetan Cookie of Everglo
                                                Ruffway Hun-Nee-Bun
CH. RUFFWAY MARPA
                                                CH. KARMA FROSTY KNIGHT OF EVERGLO
                              CH. RUFFWAY CHOGAL
                                                Ruffway Khambu
              CH. RUFFWAY KARA SHING
                                                CH. KAI SANGS CLOWN OF EVERGLO
                              CH. RUFFWAY LHOLUNG
                                                Hamilton Norden

                                                CH. HAMILTON ACHOK
                              Licos Khung La
                                                CH. LICOS NYAPSO LA
              CH. KHAM OF NORBULINGKA
                                                CH. HAMILTON SANDUPA
                              Karma Kosala
                                                CH. KARMA SANGPO
CH. KINDERLAND'S SANG-PO
                                                CH. LAS-SA-GRE'S MANCHADO DORADO
                              Dzin-Pa Rinpoche
                                                Chika Rinpoche
              Ch'ha-ha-chi
                                                CH. KEPA RINPOCHE
                              Ron-Si Rinpoche
                                                CH. TASHI RINPOCHE
</pre>

Ch. Quetzal Feyla of Kyi-Chu (D);
whelped February 27, 1963; silver
grizzle. Dr. R. J. Berndt, Owner
and Handler. Mrs. J. Amanns and
Ruth H. Smith, Breeders.

<pre>
                                            Hamilton Yangchen
                        CH. HAMILTON TATSIENLU
                                            Hamilton Novo
            CH. HAMILTON KALON
                                            Hamilton Dakmar
                        CH. HAMILTON TUGHAR
                                            Hamilton Nanning
CH. HAMILTON JIMPA
                                            Hamilton Yangchen
                        CH. HAMILTON TATSIENLU
                                            Hamilton Novo
            CH. HAMILTON SAMADA
                                            Hamilton Dakmar
                        Hamilton Lachen
                                            Takia (import)

                                            CH. LAS-SA-GRE'S MANCHADO DORADO
                        Rincan of Kelea
                                            Karma Rinpoche
            CH. COLARLIE'S SHAN BANGALOR
                                            Hsaio Ti Sambo
                        Ai Wu Ting Ling
                                            CH. FU LA SIMPATICA
CH. COLARLIE'S MISS SHANDHA
                                            CH. WU TAI
                        CH. MING TALI II, C. D.
                                            CH. MING KYI
            Miradel's Ming Fu Chia, C. D.
                                            Chuong Foo
                        CH. FU LA SIMPATICA
                                            CH. FARDALE FU SSI
</pre>

Am. and Can. Ch. Reiniet's St.
Nicholas (D); whelped December
25, 1968; golden; Group I. H. C.
and R. H. Cohrs, Reiniet's Kennels, Breeders and Owners. Elaine
Brown, Handler.

			CH. HAMILTON KALON
		Hamilton Toradga	
			CH. HAMILTON DEN-SA
	America's Sandlwood of Pamu		
			Lin-Li Poo
		Lady Pamu	
			Lo-Tsien
CH. AMERICA'S SING SONG			
			CH. HAMILTON KALON
		Hamilton Toradga	
			CH. HAMILTON DEN-SA
	America's Serpo		
			Lin-Li Poo
		Lady Pamu	
			Lo-Tsien
			Hamilton Shi-Pon
		CH. KARMA KUSHOG	
			CH. HAMILTON KARMA
	CH. ZIJUH TSAM		
			CH. HAMILTON SANDUPA
		CH. HAMILTON SHIM-TRU	
			Hamilton Saung
Reiniet's Yserral-Pa			
			CH. LA MIA'S EL REYECITO
		Cha-Lia's Rimshi Kyipup Kye	
			Lui-Gi's Kypti Kye of Cha-Lia
	Reiniet's Ai Khan Tu		
			CH. LA MIA'S EL REYECITO
		Cito's Manyusu Gyalma of Reico	
			Lui-Gi's Kypti Kye of Cha-Lia

Ch. Ruffway Mashaka (D); whelped July 29, 1968; golden; Best in Show. Robert and Georgia Palmer, Ruffway Kennels, Breeders, Owners, and Handlers. Dr. R. J. Berndt, Judge.

<pre>
                                                            Las-Sa-Gre's Hijo D'Altiro
                                        Glenn Pines Chagpo-Ri
                                                            CH. MIRADEL'S NIMA
                        CH. KAI SANGS CLOWN OF EVERGLO
                                                            CH. LAS-SA-GRE'S MANCHADO DORADO
                                        Kai Sang Tzi-Ren of Miradel
                                                            Chika Rinpoche
CH. EVERGLO'S SPARK OF GOLD
                                                            Glen Pines Chagpo-Ri
                                        CH. KAI SANGS CLOWN OF EVERGLO
                                                            Kai Sang Tzi-Ren of Miradel
                        Tibetan Cookie of Everglo
                                                            CH. MIRADEL'S MING FU TZU
                                        Ruffway's Hun-Nee-Bun
                                                            CH. GLENFLO'S GIRJE

                                                            CH. KARMA KUSHOG
                                        CH. KARMA FROSTY KNIGHT OF EVERGLO
                                                            CH. HAMILTON SHA-TRU
                        CH. RUFFWAY CHOGAL
                                                            Cubbi Kyeri of Everglo
                                        Ruffway Khambu
                                                            Stittig's Moka Kara Deimar
CH. RUFFWAY KARA SHING
                                                            Glenn Pines Chagpo-Ri
                                        CH. KAI SANGS CLOWN OF EVERGLO
                                                            Kai Sang Tzi-Ren of Miradel
                        CH. RUFFWAY LHOLUNG
                                                            CH. HAMILTON SANDUPA
                                        Hamilton Norden
                                                            CH. HAMILTON DEN-SA
</pre>

Ch. Stonewall's Gung Ho (D); whelped April 5, 1968; golden; Group I. Mrs. Carol M. Ellsworth, Stonewall Kennels, Owner.

CH. ORLANE'S MING KYI

    CH. EVERGLO'S SPARK OF GOLD

        CH. KAI SANGS CLOWN OF EVERGLO

            Glen Pines Chagpo-Ri

            Kai Sangs Tzi-Ren of Miradel

        Tibetan Cookie of Everglo

            CH. KAI SANGS CLOWN OF EVERGLO

            Ruffway's Hun-Nee-Bun

    CH. KAI SANGS FLAME OF EVERGLO

        CH. KAI SANGS CLOWN OF EVERGLO

            Glen Pines Chagpo-Ri

            Kai Sangs Tzi-Ren of Miradel

        Hamilton Norden

            CH. HAMILTON SANDUPA

            CH. HAMILTON DEN-SA

Orlane's Su Lin

    CH. EVERGLO'S SPARK OF GOLD

        CH. KAI SANGS CLOWN OF EVERGLO

            Glen Pines Chagpo-Ri

            Kai Sangs Tzi-Ren of Miradel

        Tibetan Cookie of Everglo

            CH. KAI SANGS CLOWN OF EVERGLO

            Ruffway's Hun-Nee-Bun

    CH. ORLANE'S CHITRA OF RUFFWAY

        CH. KARMA FROSTY KNIGHT OF EVERGLO

            CH. KARMA KUSHOG

            CH. HAMILTON SHA-TRU

        Ruffway Khambu

            Cubbi Kyeri of Everglo

            Stittig's Moka-Kara Deimar

Ch. Tibet of Cornwallis (D); whelped March 16, 1966; golden; Best in Show. Mr. and Mrs. Norman Herbel, Tabu Kennels, Owners. Paul Williams, Breeder.

<pre>
                                                           CH. HAMILTON TATSIENLU
                                         CH. HAMILTON SANDUPA
                                                           Hamilton Docheno
                     Karma Yon-Ton
                                                           Hamilton Shi-Pon
                                         Karma Zurwang
                                                           Karma Tara   .
  Karma Tharpa
                                                           CH. HAMILTON CHANG-TANG
                                         Americal's Sandar of Pamu
                                                           Lady Pamu
                     Karma Kam-Bu
                                                           Hamilton Toradga
                                         Hamilton Khib-Tru
                                                           Hamilton Nirvana

                                                           CH. HAMILTON TATSIENLU
                                         CH. HAMILTON ACHOK
                                                           Hamilton Dobra
                     CH. LICOS CHAPLIA LA
                                                           CH. AMERICAL'S LENG KONG
                                         CH. LICOS KARO LA
                                                           CH. AMERICAL'S RIKA
  CH. LICOS CHETI LA
                                                           CH. HAMILTON TSANG
                                         CH. AMERICAL'S LENG KONG
                                                           Hamilton Suchau
                     CH. LICOS NYAPSO LA
                                                           CH. HAMILTON TSANG
                                         CH. AMERICAL'S RIKA
                                                           CH. HAMILTON TORMA
</pre>